APOCALYPSE CHILD

APOCALYPSE CHILD

A LIFE IN END TIMES

A Memoir

FLOR EDWARDS

Turner Publishing Company
Nashville, Tennessee
New York, New York
www.turnerpublishing.com

Cover design: Maddie Cothren
Cover artwork: Jesse Lucas
Book design: Glen Edelstein
Author Photo: Jasmin Kuhn

Library of Congress Cataloging-in-Publication Data
Names: Edwards, Flor, author.
Title: Apocalypse child : a life in end times : a memoir / Flor Edwards.
Description: Nashville, Tennessee : Turner Publishing Company, 2018.
Identifiers: LCCN 2017055998 | ISBN 9781683367680 (pbk. : alk. paper)
Subjects: LCSH: Edwards, Flor. | Family International
   (Organization)--Biography.
Classification: LCC BP605.C38 E39 2018 | DDC 299/.93 [B] --dc23
LC record available at https://lccn.loc.gov/2017055998

Printed in the United States of America
18 19 20 10 9 8 7 6 5 4 3 2 1

Everything is ceremony
in the wild garden of childhood.
—*Pablo Neruda*

Looking back, I can say with certainty,
that beyond the madness, yet amidst the chaos,
it was a magical childhood. The only thing certain about
childhood is that it begins with magic.

APOCALYPSE CHILD

PROLOGUE

SHORTLY AFTER MY SEVENTH BIRTHDAY and before the monsoon season came that year, Tamar, my twin sister, and I took to killing butterflies for fun. We didn't know that every time we rubbed the powder off their wings we played God, shortening their lifespan by days, which, for a butterfly, means years.

From our limited knowledge of science, which we'd learned from encyclopedias, we knew that butterflies only had six weeks to live, so when we succeeded in catching one, we transferred it to a glass jar and thoroughly inspected its minute details—the long spindly legs, the sparkly iridescence of the wings, the waving intuitive antennae—as if by keeping it contained we could somehow prolong its delicate life.

"Look," Tamar told me, holding a mature monarch by its spongy body so as not to tamper with its wings, "their wings are identical, just like us." I examined the black veins that broke through the butterfly's deep orange, canvas-like wings, a fire-red map of the Amazon River I'd seen under *B*, for Brazil.

I nodded. Just like us.

Sometimes the butterfly escaped through the thatches of the woven bamboo net. Sometimes the butterfly disappeared, as if by magic, and we moved on to our next captive. We were predators. Most often we killed the butterfly, rubbing the powder off its wings until they were paper-thin and see-through—six weeks of caterpillar metamorphosis shattered in an instant.

Afterward, we conducted an elaborate funeral on a nearby hill that sloped up to the base of a high wall surrounding the yard. I knew the walls were there so no one could see in and to keep us safe inside. High walls surrounded every home I had lived in. At the top were loops of barbed wire or jagged glass etched into the cement so no one could climb over.

The butterfly funerals were a grand procession complete with old black shoeboxes in which to lay the fallen insects, prayers, Bible verses and poems written on crumpled pieces of paper, and small wooden crosses patched together with twine. We chose our burial site atop a grassy knoll under a baby palm tree that sprouted a relief of shade from the merciless sun. After adorning the makeshift grave with exotic wildflowers—orchids and poppies, hibiscus and honey-suckle—and blankets of fern, we sent the butterfly with a sigh of guilt to its unknown afterlife, a life as clandestine and enigmatic as the creature itself.

All I knew about the afterlife I had learned from Father David. He was the leader who would guide us, like Moses, into the End Time, a period that was fast approaching and was predicted in the Bible, in the book of Revelation. He said I was a chosen child of

God, and I was to be God's End Time soldier. He was God's chosen prophet, preparing us to save the world from the Great Apocalypse, which would come in 1993, when I would be twelve years old. Father David claimed to be the mouthpiece of God. He lived in hiding with an entourage of followers, including his wife, Maria, and his son, Davidito, "Little David." He sat on his throne in his top-secret hideout, predicting our future and deciding our fate—a fate that included possible martyrdom and certain premature death.

The gate separating our yard from the dirt road outside was boarded with wood. I knew I wasn't allowed to leave or I would be punished—or worse, consumed by the wickedness of the world. In the afternoon, when the sun softened its rays, we were allowed to go outside for one hour as long as we stayed within the perimeters of the walls.

Besides keeping us safe, I knew that the walls were also there to keep the evil spirits out. I became fascinated with this Spirit World that could not be seen or felt but only experienced through some unknown sense—a sense I believed I was developing keenly, an awareness that was becoming as acute and sharp as my physical senses. A sense that had slowly, over time, overridden my capabilities of reason or logic.

During recess, when no one was looking, I pressed my nose against the metal bars of the gate and searched for other signs of life. I found a tiny crack in the wall and stared through the peephole. I saw a slow-moving rickshaw, or a shimmering snake, or a mother carrying a child on her back while balancing a bucket on her head. The beauty I saw, within the walls and without, was enough to turn my heart inside out.

If the evil spirits hid in living creatures, like Father David said, I thought they must be beautiful. And surely they mustn't be as dangerous as he had led us to believe. Maybe it was that year when I began to wonder what it would be like to live outside, among the host of evil spirits, instead of safe and protected within the walls.

CHAPTER 1

ONE NIGHT WHEN I WAS five, Mom came to my bedside and told me I was special. "You are a chosen child of God," she said. "We don't always know the reason for God's will, but he has one." She placed one hand on my heart and taped a Bible verse to the wall beside my bed. "God will never give you any temptation greater than you can bear," she said softly. She kissed my forehead. When she got up to leave the room, the sharp, sweet smell of her lingered long after. She and Dad weren't always around anymore, and I often longed for the days when they had been, when we had been together as a family.

I knew that by *temptation* Mom meant the moment of death. And I knew that because I was born into the Children of God, I was born to bring light to the world before the Great Apocalypse. I was never told I could be anything other than a martyr for God when I grew up.

■ ■

OTHER THAN RECRUITING SOULS OR singing and preaching God's word on the streets of California, I don't remember Mom or Dad ever having a real job. Now that we lived in Thailand Mom came to my bed at night to tell me the story of how I was born, or how she met Dad in Spain after she had joined the Children of God, a group that claimed to be on a mission to save the world and whose members called themselves "missionaries."

Dad, Mom told me, gave up pursuing a degree at one of America's top universities to join the Children of God. America, where my dad was from, was evil, I knew from Father David's letters, which doomed the Western world. "God had a greater plan for your father," Mom said. "God has a greater plan for *all* his children." Mom never liked money, nor did she see herself as fit to have any, which is probably why she adapted so well to the life of a missionary. Many members who joined the Children of God came from broken families. Maybe that's what broken people do; they bond together to fix things.

Mom was born and raised in Malmo, Sweden, to a Danish father who often came home in the early afternoons drunk, she'd say, and a Swedish mother—a woman she called "simple" and whom I never knew well. Mom, who called herself Mercy in the Children of God, told me stories of herself as a young girl, how her parents dropped her off every Sunday at a Lutheran church with her younger sister, Eva. Mom loved the sermons and excelled in church activities, eventually becoming a Girl Scout leader. As a teenager she was a traveler and full of adventure. Her stories made me think of how brave she must've been—traversing the Swedish slopes, getting caught in a blizzard while skiing, bravely crossing a narrow bridge that swung high above a Norwegian fjord on a dare from one of her boyfriends. And she was beautiful, with olive skin, slender fingers, long brunette hair, deep-set eyes, and a bright, natural smile.

One day, on her way to buy a ticket to Tunisia in search of some unknown adventure, Mom met Thomas, a man she describes as "having eyes that were full of light." From the stories she tells he glowed with an aura she had never seen. He sat on a street corner near a bustling train station strumming a guitar. She sat down next to him, and he told her about Jesus. He invited her to come to his house for dinner. He lived with a group of other people, and they followed orders from a leader they called Father David. Father David lived on a ranch in Texas and communicated with his followers in long, elaborate letters that quoted and interpreted Biblical scripture. Mom never asked details about Father David's whereabouts or if she would ever meet him. She knew these people were living their lives with purpose. That same night, she left her fiancé and her old life in Sweden to follow this enigmatic leader and join the eclectic group that called itself the Children of God.

My dad, although also adventurous, was more inclined to a sense of daring achievement and insatiable curiosity. His large, Irish-Catholic family from South Pasadena was split when he was nine and his parents divorced. As a teenager he spent weekends camping in the High Sierras with his dog, a German shepherd–collie mix named D-O-G that was so smart, Dad said, they had to remind him he was a dog every time they called his name. A geology student at the top of his class at the University of California, Davis, Dad quit his studies weeks before graduating to follow his five older siblings in joining the Children of God, a movement that had swept through California. It was a decision he never regretted.

■ ■

NEITHER I NOR MY PARENTS ever met Father David or knew what he looked like, but if you'd asked me in my earlier years to tell you the story of the Children of God's humble beginnings, I'd have recited it to you like it was holier than all scripture.

On a California evening in 1968, a man named David Brandt Berg walked along the Huntington Beach Pier. He had been born in Oakland, California, in 1919, ten years before the great stock market crash. He'd been a preacher in Arizona, but had quarreled with the ministry and struck out alone. On this day he wore a French beret, slacks, formal shoes, and a blue sweater. He tucked his hands into his pockets and held his head low, contemplating his forty-nine years. His shoes kicked up dust. The streets were dark. Lampposts on sidewalks cast amber spells that elongated the shadows. Hippies huddled together on the street corners or wandered alone, their heads bowed. On the beach, searchers dotted the sandy shores. As night settled, David Berg had an epiphany. Even though there were many people around him, Berg saw that they were lonely and afraid.

A blinding light flashed before his eyes. He heard what he claimed to be the voice of God—loud, clear, and articulate. For a moment all was still. "Wilt thou become 'King of the Beggars'?" the voice said.

At nearly fifty years old, David Berg had found his life's mission. The hippies around him were lost, and it was his job to save them. They were searching for a way out of "the system," and he had the answers to their questions. He believed that the problem of the young hippie generation was that they lacked purpose and meaning in life. His solution was to band them together and save the world from damnation and hell. David Berg, along with his wife, Eve, and their four young children, Deborah, Aaron, Ho, and Faithy, began gathering the outcasts—the downtrodden, the drug addicts, the lost souls. They formed a singing group called Teens for Christ and began performing at nightclubs, music festivals, and hot hangouts. Berg's aging evangelical-minister mother made peanut butter sandwiches every day for the hippies on the pier. The Teens for Christ took over a coffee shop called the Light Club at 116 Main Street and began hosting daily Bible studies and occasional betrothals.

Father David teamed up with famed TV evangelist Fred Jordan in Los Angeles. Jordan would become Berg's mentor in a partnership that lasted fifteen years. Jordan offered Berg's new movement use of his mission building at the corner of 5th Street and Towne Avenue in downtown L.A., near Skid Row. The Children of God took over the five-story building and were soon heading a mission to alert Americans to the "End Time." Members passed out literature on the street warning of the impending doom. They staged vigilant protests against traditional Christian churches. Dressed in sackcloth, carrying thick wooden staves, and with ashes smeared on their foreheads, they stormed into Sunday morning services to warn congregations of the Great Apocalypse. Most of these sessions ended in arrest and a headline in the newspaper the next morning. The Children of God, which also called itself the Family, quickly captured the attention of the media and frequently made front-page news. In 1971 they graced the cover of *Time* magazine, which hailed the movement as "The Jesus Revolution," with a cover story titled "The Alternative Jesus: Psychedelic Christ." Members traveled throughout the United States, inviting others to join them in their quest for freedom, redemption, and salvation in preparation for the Great Apocalypse.

My twin sister, Tamar, claims it was the riots, the assassinations, and the Vietnam War that gave rise to the counterculture movement we were born into. I always held that it was the Indians. If they hadn't come into young Father David's Arizona parish barefoot, he would never have felt compelled to offer them salvation. Then he would never have been banned from his church for inviting them into his service and never would have started his own new religion.

■ ■

SHORTLY AFTER THE CHILDREN OF God was founded on Huntington Beach and spread throughout the United States, Father David sent out members he called "missionaries" to start new missions in locations all over the world, starting in Europe and spreading eventually to Asia, Africa, and South America. According to my Auntie Julie's account, my Uncle Bird was the first of my dad's siblings to join the Children of God in California. Uncle Bird's real name was Francis. He was a talented musician who wrote songs and had the voice of an angel. A gentle soul, he spent some time camping in the High Sierras searching for his life's calling. As my dad tells it, during the week after the 1971 Sylmar earthquake, in San Fernando, Uncle Bird came home and started talking about the people who lived in a big building on Skid Row. They were doing good things, he said: passing out goods to the homeless, helping those who had lost everything in the earthquake, getting young people off drugs and "high on Jesus" (as he put it).

My Uncle Dust, the eldest brother of my dad's siblings, intended to talk his little brother out of joining the group. But then he remembered a commitment he'd made to God while on the battlefield in Vietnam. Uncle Dust had a fine arm for baseball but had been drafted soon after making the minor-league team for the San Francisco Giants. While out with his platoon one day on a ground mission, he stepped into the bushes to pee. He heard some blasts, and when he came out all his comrades were dead. He realized he had lived through a miracle. He made up his mind to dedicate his life to God.

Uncle Dust, Auntie Julie, and Uncle Bird joined the Children of God together that day. Having natural leadership skills and experience training soldiers, Uncle Dust soon became a high-ranking leader. Two more siblings joined. Dad was the last of his siblings to join, in 1978. He wrote a letter to Uncle Dust, who was living with his wife, Mahayla, in Spain, informing Uncle Dust of his decision to join. Uncle Dust invited Dad to move to Spain and be part of the exciting mission there. The Children of God was now sending missionaries all over the world and they were expanding rapidly in Europe. Living in that house with Uncle Dust and Mahayla was Mom.

Mom said she joined because Father David offered the youth of her generation a purpose in life and a way to serve God without joining the church. She'd followed the movement to Denmark, where she met Uncle Dust and Mahayla, and then moved with them to Majorca, Spain. They lived in a villa near the ocean that had been leased to them at reduced rent. Mom and Dad were sent out to gather food for the group. Since neither spoke Spanish, and Mom barely spoke English, they carried a sign to inform potential donors of their names and what they needed. They visited churches to gather donations and meet potential members. They were soon collecting coffee, sugar, varieties of meats, spices, and day-old bread. Dad said they provisioned everything through their supplications, even diapers, although they didn't need them.

Mom and Dad fell in love and were married at a simple church ceremony on a pleasant August day. Mom was eight months pregnant with my oldest brother, John, and she didn't have the money to buy a traditional wedding gown; instead, she wore a brown flower-print dress that gave way for her bulging belly. Dad wore a pale blue, collared shirt under a dark brown corduroy suit. Someone threw rice on them after the ceremony as a gesture of good luck and prosperity.

While out on their missions, Mom and Dad gathered a list of potential donors. Soon they were sending out monthly newsletters to these contacts, complete with photos of their growing family. Over time the list grew to some five hundred friends, some of whom became monthly sponsors and reliable contributors. Many stayed in contact for years, and their donations became a main source of income for my parents' mission.

The Children of God were always on the move, never staying in one place for more than a few months at most. Shortly after they met in 1978, Mom and Dad moved from Spain back to Mom's hometown of Malmo, Sweden. Mom was pregnant and needed a place to settle down and have her first baby, but the travel habits of the Children of God were not conducive to rearing children. My Swedish Uncle Leif wanted nothing to do with the Children of God. Mom's mother, my Mormor, didn't think joining was a smart idea either. But members of the Children of God were encouraged to defy their parents' wishes if doing so meant serving God's highest will and following Father David's calling to save the world.

Mom's childhood church, the Mission Church of Lomma, took my parents in, and with that support, Mom and Dad soon formed a home with a man named Gibbea and his two wives, Tamar and Flor, who were also part of the Children of God. They had sixteen children altogether. (Father David encouraged multiple wives. He also condoned women forming couples with other women, but he shunned male intimacy as "sodomy.") The Swedish government paid my dad to learn

Swedish, and he earned a meager income as a part-time welder. That, along with wh at they earned from donations, was enough to start raising their young family.

When I think back on my childhood, I realize I wasn't special at all. But one thing set me apart: aside from Mom's stories of her past or the few photographs she owned, I have no memory of my ancestry or record of my lineage; there is only Father David. Most people can talk about their grandfathers and great-grandfathers; they can tell stories of how they inherited pie recipes from their grandmothers' grandmothers or how their ancestors nearly starved to death migrating to Ellis Island or died fighting for a cause in the Civil War. But not me—I have no secret family recipes; I have no noble war stories. When I picture my family tree, I see Mom with her electric smile, Dad with his balding head, and my siblings—too many to count on two hands. When I envision my ancestors I see faraway Nordic countries where fjords split the land. I see Spain, where my parents met. I see the Atlantic Ocean pooling into Mediterranean seas and European countries separated by vibrant colors, veined with rivers, picturesque and rich with culture and history. When people ask me where I'm from I see three continents—Europe to the north, Asia to the east, and North America to the west—and I am in the middle. I have no country; I have no city; I have no ancestral pride; my lineage stops at David Brandt Berg. If it weren't for him and his prophesies and visions, neither I, nor thousands of others, would ever have been born.

CHAPTER 2

ON THE NIGHT OF MY birth, Mom tells me, a prophecy was received that I was to be a bearer of light along with Tamar, who had spent nine months snug in the womb with me.

We were born on December 13, 1981—Santa Lucia day—in Malmo, Sweden, a country as big as California with a population the size of Los Angeles. Because Father David renounced birth control of any kind, Mom already had two children: John, my older brother, age two, and Mary Ann, with shiny blond hair, age one. Before the birth, Gibbea closed his eyes and had a vision. Sometimes the adults were so desperate they prayed to receive prophesies from the Spirit World to guide them through the Great Apocalypse. Gibbea laid his hands on my mother's bulging belly and started praying and speaking in tongues. He saw, with his inner eye, two girls, each holding a candle bright enough to illuminate the whole world. The world is cold and dark and in desperate need of light, he proclaimed. The final words of his prophecy foretold that "the two shall bear the light."

Mom told the story every year: The night we were born, young girls walked through the streets singing Christmas carols. They were dressed in white Grecian-style gowns that cascaded to the floor, their hair adorned with halos of holy wreaths The leader of the group wore a crown of real candles glowing on her head, and the rest of the carolers held lit candles in their hands to illuminate their path. Their long garments were decorated with blue satin sashes. They knocked on people's doors and offered to serenade them. The smell of warm, freshly baked cinnamon rolls wafted through the doorway as the carolers gently chanted traditional tunes. The music echoed through the cobblestone streets and settled on blankets of soft, fresh snow. The name *Lucia* derives from the Latin word for *light;* Santa Lucia day is also known as the Festival of Light. From the way Mom tells it, the parade of girls seemed like an angelic procession. She had a way of making me believe I was born on a heavenly day.

Mom was busy pounding dough for cinnamon rolls with one of Gibbea's wives, Tamar, when her water broke. Water gushed out of her while outside the carolers sang, "Silent night, holy night, all is calm, all is bright. Round yon virgin mother and child. . . . " It was early evening. We weren't due for another two weeks, but the doctor had warned her that early birthing was not uncommon for twins.

Mom says I was born to be a fighter because I kicked Tamar out. I was a breach baby, or as Mom used to call me, a "footling." After Tamar emerged, my foot followed and just stayed there, dangling out of her for nineteen minutes while I imagine I enjoyed the warmth of her cozy womb alone, contemplating whether I wanted to emerge since I had the great burden of bringing light to the world. The doctors had put a huge mirror in front of Mom's delivery bed so she could watch our birth. Mom saw my foot turn from soft and baby pink to a blue-purple hue. The doctors weren't sure if I would come out dead or alive. Mom had an audience of twenty-some medical students watching our birth for extra-curricular credit, taking notes on their important clipboards and wearing fancy white suits.

The morning after our birth the Malmo newspaper thought we were worth a mention since twins were uncommon and Sweden had a population of only eight million. Mom still has the newspaper clipping with a photo of her looking tired and beautiful in her white hospital gown. She is holding one twin in each arm. The only difference between us is that Tamar has a full head of hair and I came out bald as an egg. Mom named us after Gibbea's two wives, Tamar and Flor. She spotted a birthmark on my cheek and said "Flor" suited me best. "God put a flower on your face," she'd say, "so we could distinguish between the two of you." When I was old enough to draw my own conclusions, I decided the birthmark resembled a smudge of dirt or a smushed cornflake.

■ ■

GIBBEA, TAMAR, AND FLOR WHO all spoke Spanish fluently, soon left Malmo with their children to start a mission in Mexico. When Tamar and I were six months old, our family flew to Mexico to join them. When Tamar and I were a year old, my family drove from Mexico City to Eagle Rock, California, to live next to my paternal grandpa.

At dusk in Eagle Rock, a massive boulder on the city's northern edge cast a shadow the shape of an eagle over the valley of ash trees, giving the city its name. The city was surrounded by sedimentary rock and low-lying hills. During the day the sun beat down hard, and at night the Santa Monica Mountains played backdrop to a display of dazzling lights and magnificent swirls of smoggy sunset pastels.

I'd been taught from an early age to call Father David "Grandpa," but I knew perfectly well who my real grandpa was. My grandpa, a recovering alcoholic who was working to get his life together after a few failed business ventures and a career in entertainment, often muttered under his breath about what in the hell his children were doing joining a freak organization. Everyone said my grandpa was mean and had an inappropriate sense of humor called sarcasm—one time he sent a woman home from the dinner table crying because he told her she looked like a horse with her buck teeth and obnoxious nose—but for the few years that I knew him, I thought he had the sweetest face with eyes that always smiled and puffy white hair that matched his perfectly shaped mustache.

My parents needed to earn some money in California. It was a resting place to save up for our big move to Asia, home to a growing mission my parents wanted to join. From his top-secret location, Father David had begun having visions about the wickedness of Western nations. These elaborate prophecies came suddenly and unannounced in his dreams—visions of America burning in a lake of fire, of towers falling, of the dollar bill (which he called the "Green Paper Pig") exploding, of the country in all its capitalistic glory depicted as a greedy whore. He had his faithful scribe, his wife Maria, write them down and had his cartoonists sketch up drawings of the apocalyptic images. He compiled them into communiqués, which he called "MO Letters," (MO standing for 'Moses' since, like Moses in the Bible, he was going to lead us into the 'Promised Land' of heaven after the Apocalypse) and had them printed and distributed en masse to his followers. In his letters, Father David ordered his followers to set their sights on third-world countries, where people were destitute and hungry for salvation, ready to hear our message of the End Time and the Great Apocalypse. It was our job to guarantee everyone a spot in heaven. By the time I was born, Father David had twelve thousand followers living in tight-knit communities, compounds we called "homes," scattered across the world.

In California, Mom and Dad started busking, a practice that intermittently became our family's primary source of income. Mom still has a photograph of Dad squatting on the sidewalk at the Paramount Swap Meet in Los Angeles with a guitar on his knee. A guitar case on the ground next to him holds a few tossed-in coins and dollar bills. There was a large cardboard sign with handwritten block letters reading, in Spanish, "*missionaries. . . a Tailandia.*" John, my oldest brother, stands next to him with his black hair mopped over his head, wearing a flannel checkered shirt, suspenders, and corduroy pants, belting his heart out. Mary Ann, my older sister, sleeps in the back of the navy-blue buggy that was big enough to fit all four of us kids at one time. Her blond hair is combed back into pigtails. Mom hands someone a colorful poster of Heaven. A man walks by. Someone else tosses a coin into the guitar case. Tamar and I are perched in the front of the buggy, wearing matching baby-blue dresses dotted with white daisies.

Mom went a year after she had us before getting pregnant again. Heidi was born in a hospital in San Luis Obispo on November 22, 1983. She was a willful, stubborn child with fire-red hair. She refused to participate in family photos and always threw a fit when she wanted her pacifier.

William Frederick Edwards was born on New Year's Eve a year later in a West Los Angeles hospital. With soft brown curls, pudgy cheeks, a dimpled chin, and inquisitive, light-brown eyes, he was adorable but mean. Defiant and willful, his first word was "No!" but it came out sounding like "Nawt!" When he was a toddler he used to form his fingers into the shape of a gun and pretend to shoot people for no apparent reason.

As William's due date approached, I asked Mom if we would throw Heidi in the trash can to make room for the new baby. There were already five of us. I didn't know I would have to make room for seven more.

CHAPTER 3

When I first heard the news, Mom was working out to a Jane Fonda exercise video. She wore a pink and red striped leotard, grey leggings, and white tights—Jane Fonda, not Mom. Mom never wore such revealing clothing. Auntie Mary was busy in the kitchen boiling chicken for dinner. Tamar and I were copying Mom, lying on our backs and lifting and squeezing our legs in time with the big-haired enthusiast onscreen. Our nameless dollies lay next to us. They never left our sides.

"News flash!" Auntie Mary came running into the living room wearing her white and black checkered apron. Her thin hair was tied back into a little bun. Her pants were rolled up to reveal her thick calves. She held one of Father David's MO Letters. It smelled of fresh ink. She flipped through the pages and landed on a picture of a masculine woman wearing the same spiky crown that rests atop the head of the Statue of Liberty. She looked selfish, egocentric. The woman's legs were spread open, and she held a globe of the world in one hand. In her other hand, at the mercy of her wrath, rested a group of poverty-stricken third-world folks. In between her legs stood various prestigious buildings, such as the Pentagon and the White House, representing lust, sloth, and greed.

"This is so exciting!" Auntie Mary said with a lisp. Her eyes widened. She pursed her lips and began reading the words of her prophet.

The world was ending soon, Father David said, and the United States would be a less than optimal place to live during the Great Apocalypse. The woman in the picture represented "America the Whore," and we must flee all Western nations. We were destined for Southeast Asia. We'd saved enough money. I could tell that Mom and Dad were thrilled.

Happily, I could bring my dolly. She was hard and hollow. The lines carved in her head meant she had real hair. Her hands had intricate details of fingers and toes, including the outlines of nails. On her thumb was a black dot from the time a bee landed on her hand and stung her, I swore.

"This is so exciting!" Mom agreed with her sister-in-law. "One of God's adventures."

■ ■

FOR THE MONTHS BEFORE WE moved "out East," as my parents referred to our Asian destination, we traveled along California's coastlines, residing in tents and trailers in campgrounds in Malibu, San Luis Obispo, and Pismo Beach. Sometimes when we ran out of campgrounds to stay at, we stayed in the home of my

Aunt Mary and Uncle Nick and their five children. We stopped to beg people for money whenever we neared a shopping center. We weren't the family dressed in rags looking cold and dirty, holding out cans and asking for money. There was a lightness to our begging. We dressed neatly. Mom's electric smile was infectious. Her eyes shone brightly. She wore the perfect shade of lipstick and a turquoise eye shadow that brought out her eyes, which always sparkled.

The Children of God had a way of fitting God into their begging, and it turned the act of imploring into a practice they called "witnessing." We witnessed in shopping malls and on street corners. We witnessed in parks and state campgrounds. We witnessed in restaurants and on public transportation—buses, trains, and airplanes. During Christmas season, we and our cousins dressed up—the girls as angels and the boys as shepherds—and sang Christmas carols in the center court of the mall in front of JCPenney. Santa Claus was there with his cotton-white hair and overstuffed belly. I was suspicious of Santa. I refused to request any gifts but reluctantly sat on his lap so I could have a cookie. I loved cookies. I loved the taste of ginger and cinnamon and sugar and the way the plastic crinkled every time I opened the package to find the surprise of plump raisins scattered throughout. The crumbs disintegrated and soiled the collar of my angelic costume, but maintaining a heavenly appearance wasn't as important as appreciating every morsel.

Our open guitar case lay in front of us. We sang until it didn't seem as if we were begging at all. During the day, when we weren't busking or witnessing, we played in beds of pine needles that had fallen from the sequoias that towered above our camp. We gathered pinecones as big as my cousin Talkee's head and built forts with fallen petrified logs. At night Dad played us a song before bed. He plucked gently at the strings of his old Fender guitar and sang,

If I have not Charity,
If Love doesn't flow from me,
I am no-othing,
Jesus reduce me to Love.

The stars came out, and I dozed off to his soft, sweet voice. When it was time to move, we packed up our things and found another temporary living space.

■ ■

MOM WAS PREGNANT AGAIN WITH child number seven. We were living with my aunt and uncle in Eagle Rock. Mom spent the evenings sewing us girls matching outfits—turquoise dresses dotted with orange and yellow flowers that stopped just above our knees and had straps that tied over our shoulders. A few nights before we were due to leave, I was awakened in the middle of the night to a commotion in the hallway.

"Mercy's bleeding." I heard my Auntie Mary's voice amid the muffled whispers. "It's serious and she won't stop."

"Make her lie down," Dad urged. Blood was gushing out of her. Auntie Mary laid plastic lining on the bed so she wouldn't stain the white sheets. I saw Mom lying with her knees bent and her feet in a pool of blood. We kids were rounded up and told to stay still and be quiet. I didn't want Mom to die.

"It looks like she's going to lose the baby," Auntie Mary whispered frantically. "Don't let the children know." But we knew. Mom was rushed to the hospital, and we were told to go back to bed. That night she delivered her first stillborn, a boy.

Days later we boarded a plane headed for Thailand. The night before we left, Mom braided our hair and laid out our shoes by the door—sandals with thick rubber soles and strong metal buckles.

When we arrived at the airport for our departure, it was dark and close to midnight. I pressed my face against the large glass window overlooking the tarmac. I watched the planes as they taxied and landed. I was still in shock over the incident a few nights earlier. Everything was going to change once we moved to the East, Father David said. We were God's ambassadors on a mission to save the world before the Great Apocalypse in 1993. I was thrilled by the idea of a new adventure, and I could tell that my parents were too. Even though Mom had just suffered a miscarriage, she was, on the outside, back to her normal self, humming scriptural tunes and praising the Lord as we made our preparations for the big move.

We arrived at Bangkok International Airport in late September of 1986, just in time for John's seventh birthday—two parents and six children dressed in matching outfits, looking like a modern-day von Trapp family.

CHAPTER 4

WHEN WE GOT OFF THE plane I heard the muffled sound of a language I couldn't understand. People walked slowly and stared at us as if we were aliens. "*Fa-fat falang,*" they'd say, pointing to Tamar and me—"foreigner twins."

Mom pushed the same blue buggy she'd pushed Tamar and me in when our family sang on the streets in California, but this time Heidi and William shared the front and Tamar and I walked at its side holding on to the metal bars.

We picked up our few pieces of luggage and made our way out of the terminal and onto the streets. Women stopped their chores to stare. They wore flower-print sarongs and plain-colored shirts, their hair tied back in taut buns, their half-naked children playing near the sewer. The smell of steamed white rice and fish-bone soup with lemongrass filled the air. It was early morning, and the sun was starting to peek through a thick layer of clouds. There was a cacophony of sounds. Street vendors clanged their thin copper pots. Peddlers shouted bargains in Thai and broken English, each trying to outdo the other. Roosters cackled on the sides of dusty roads. Car horns honked endlessly. Somewhere in the background I heard a radio blasting the lyrics,

> Someone told me long ago
> There's a calm before the storm
> I know it's been comin' for some time
> . . . .
> I want to know, have you ever seen the rain
> Comin' down on a sunny day?

I held on tight to the stroller. Tamar and I turned to each other and laughed. We thought it was funny that the singer said "lain" instead of "rain." Dark, nebulous clouds hung low in the sky. The air was hot and thick, like you could slice your hand through it and make a dent.

Dad was already sweating from the humidity, and his white shirt clung to his torso. He had instructions from one of the leaders on how to get to our new home in Bangkok. He flagged down a *song tao,* a large, open-air taxi that would take us to our new home, where three to four other families—twenty to thirty people in all—lived. The Children of God did not believe in birth control, and the children now outnumbered the adults three to one. We would be living in large, commune-style homes with up to thirty or fifty other members. Most had relocated to Southeast Asia at Father David's and the other leaders' orders. (Similarly, multifamily compounds had been established in South America.)

The leaders designated who lived where, and the instructions were passed on to us through top-secret letters.

We arrived at a home with grey cement walls and a large metal gate. I noticed that the gate was boarded with plywood; the setting was much different from the open-air campgrounds I had been used to when we traveled along the coast in California.

Someone who was called a "home shepherd" led us on a quick tour. A large dining hall housed rows and rows of tables and wooden benches. An open doorway led to a communal-style kitchen with multiple stovetops and lots of open storage space. Cabinets marked with labels stored large barrels of bulk supplies and stacks and stacks of color-coded dishes.

As we walked through the cramped halls, I noticed that the bedrooms were filled with bunk beds and mattresses on the floor, more beds than the rooms had probably been designed for. The bed sheets were stretched tightly across the mattresses, with not a single wrinkle, as if someone had spent a long time making them perfect and stiff, like a board. The wide-paned windows over-looked a large grassy yard, and there were many children playing outside, more than I had been used to being around in California.

Having just arrived, we six kids were shown a room where we could sleep. Dad had told us on the plane that the time zones were different here on the opposite side of the world. We were a good sixteen hours ahead of California, he said, so we would be "jet-lagged."

"Sleep up," Mom agreed. "You'll need the rest."

We slept on thin foam mattresses sprawled across the floor for what seemed like days. We woke up together and began crying simultaneously, unfamiliar with the humidity of the dark, thick air. Then we fell back asleep, adjusting to the jet lag and the pollution that stung our eyes and made it difficult to breathe. We slept sporadically and intuitively, giving no thought to time or schedule. When we were finally ready to wake, we were greeted by faces I had never seen before.

One adult wore light beige shorts and a Hawaiian-print shirt with red flowers. His blue flip-flops clacked against his heels every time he took a step. He wore thin glasses and had wispy, light brown hair. He smiled widely for no reason at all. Mom welcomed him with a hug. I disliked her affection for him. The women in the home had long hair and wore thin sarongs that flapped open when they walked fast. Everyone dressed minimally. The men were happy. Everyone praised the Lord and shouted, "Hallelujah." I could tell there was a new enthusiasm about life and God that I hadn't been accustomed to in California. I was going to have to learn.

It was morning. We followed the others downstairs to the dining hall, where we found small bowls of rice cereal on the breakfast table. We ate spoonfuls of the porridge thickened with powdered milk and dark cane sugar. The rice was lumpy and the milk was sweet and tasted good. Mom and Dad were in a room with other adults praying and hearing news from Father David. I suddenly felt alone in my new home.

That afternoon we were told we could go outside to play with the other children for recess. Mary Ann found a small play-house made of wood and painted a bright blue, the color of the sky on a clear day. Mary Ann, Tamar, Heidi, William, and I managed to squeeze all five of us together into the little house. We played in it for hours as the sky transformed from cloudy with iridescent lining to grey and ominous, threatening rain or a monsoon. We took turns playing housekeeper. When it was Heidi's turn, she pushed open the rectangular window-door, peeked her head out, and announced that the hut had been transformed into a restaurant. We paid her with large hollow seeds. She served us hearty portions of muddy clay wrapped in sturdy banana-leaf plates.

■ ■

THE COMPOUND IN BANGKOK WAS only a temporary home. Because of its central location, Bangkok was a holding place for families arriving in Thailand. Soon the General Area Shepherds (GAS), the area leaders in Bangkok in charge of relocating the growing number of families arriving in Southeast Asia, transferred us to Udon Thani, a city located in a northern province of Thailand, to open a new home there.

The northern region of the country was known for its lush rainforests and rural villages. We would be living there with a couple named Simon and Ecclesia and their two kids, Adam and Anaik. Other families would likely be coming and going, we were told, but our two families would be the mainstay of this new home. Soon, moving every four to six months would become routine and expected. It was exhausting.

We took public transportation to Udon Thani. Our new home, a house painted blue with sturdy wooden frames and a green and white awning, had a small cement play area in the backyard. I was excited to meet Anaik, a new friend with long dark hair and thick lashes.

In the village slums, Thai families huddled together in shacks, the old men hunched over, squatting in the same position for hours on end. The women were always beating something, either an old rug or a concoction of spices and herbs for dinner. Chickens ran freely and tackled each other over food, the vibrantly colored roosters declared their manhood by pecking the heads of the less colorful hens until they were bald and unattractive and submissive. Children ran around bare-bummed and naked-footed, their dimpled bottoms resting on the same dirt road where car tires tread.

CHAPTER 5

Oᴜᴛꜱɪᴅᴇ ᴛʜᴇ ᴡᴀʟʟꜱ, ᴅɪʀᴛ ᴡᴀꜱ everywhere. Whenever we left the compound, it crept into shoes and gathered in noses. It stuck to our skin and matted our hair. It billowed up in clouds on the side of earthen roads and turned car metal to rust. It settled into dust behind clanging rickshaws and covered the fruits and vegetables of the produce vendors, who wore sedge hats with flat tops and long-sleeved white cotton shirts with frog buttons. They stood at their fruit stands or rowed their boats along the water markets in the murky Mekong River canals. Dust spanned the horizon as far as the eye could see. It kicked up an afternoon haze that shaded the sun, and when monsoon came, thick raindrops turned the dusty roads into mud.

We left the compound only to win lost souls or gather dona-tions or take long walks in the late afternoon. Inside the walls our surroundings were almost hospital-clean, with bright white walls and spotless wood floors. The kitchen was orderly, with dishes stacked neatly and washing basins that smelled of disinfectant or Pine-Sol. The food cupboards and bulk food barrels were labeled with block letters in black marker on white masking tape. Even though we didn't own a lot of clothes and mostly wore hand-me-downs or donated garments, the clothes we had smelled like fresh laundry powder and sun from being hand- or stomp-washed and laid out to dry.

In the corner of the dining room was a fish tank that could hardly be called an aquarium because the fish inside were so ugly. It wasn't bright and cheery like an aquarium you might see in a fancy restaurant or a five-star hotel. The fish it housed were grey and dark and the water was murky, like something you'd find at the bottom of the sea or underneath the rocks off the coast of the Philippines. Two suckerfish that looked like miniature sharks latched onto the glass and sucked up anything that got in their way. Supposedly they kept the tank clean and even ate their own excrement after devouring that of every other creature in the tank. There was a crawfish that looked like a pink lobster and a couple of grey guppies. Sometimes the guppies disappeared for no apparent reason, and we cleaned out the tank and dumped in a fresh new batch.

Since the tap water wasn't safe to drink, we had to bleach or boil it. We ordered heavy five-gallon jugs of water for fifteen baht apiece and refilled them weekly. Next to the water cooler was a little bottle of bleach with a screw-on top. John was in charge of adding bleach to the bottled water. For every barrel, he added ten drops. When one barrel was finished, I watched as he care-fully counted out the bleach droplets as they disappeared into the barrel's mouth and dissolved in the water below. When John wasn't around, someone who wasn't used to dropping the bleach in the water would do it. Sometimes they accidentally let too much in, and the water burned with the bitter taste of bleach for the rest of the day. Sometimes when that happened we had to waste a whole barrel of water, but when we did drink it I figured the extra bleach kept my insides clean and in top-notch condition.

Members were only allowed to use three squares of toilet paper per trip to the toilet, and usually it was thin and cardboard-like, not "angel soft and safe for babies' bottoms." I would cheat and use five, or else I'd squat down and splash cold water between my legs; but never *ever* would I dare use six pieces of toilet paper. I knew that disobeying the words of Father David was worse than blasphemy; it was punishable by eternal damnation.

■ ■

WE HAD A LOOSE ROUTINE that involved morning prayer and Word Time—when we'd read scripture or letters from Father David—followed in the afternoon by chores, lunch, playtime, and light schooling—reading, writing, and arithmetic taught through books and educational videos. Dad was often out gathering donations and witnessing with Uncle Simon or Auntie Ecclesia. Mom stayed home and took care of us kids. She loved the adventure of this exotic rural life. In the middle of the afternoon, when the sun turned hazy and low clouds loomed on the horizon, she told us to put on our walking shoes and a long-sleeved shirt to protect our skin from the sun that seemed to beat down even beyond the layer of thick clouds. "We're going for a long walk," she announced, and then she'd give us our three options—the ditch, the bridge, or the manger—each more grueling than the last.

The ditch sloped down into a bank and had high walls of swirling red clay. When I walked inside it I felt like I was inside a giant scoop of brilliant, swirled ice cream. From the bridge, I had a perfect view of the ditch. It was a rusty color and had a structure similar to that of one of the bridges that towered over the bay of San Francisco. But our absolute favorite destination was the manger. It took us the longest to get there, but once we arrived we were in the middle of the wilderness with nothing around but dirt and the occasional tree stripped of its branches. Perched on a hollow log, the stump of a tree sat sideways, and it had a perfectly hollowed cradle, the exact size of a newborn baby. Mom managed to convince us that it was the actual manger of Baby Jesus.

We'd walk for hours. For Mom, a walk wasn't a walk unless your feet ached, blisters bubbled up on your heels, and your skin was one degree from being completely scorched. She loved to exercise. She said that's what kept her healthy and able to deliver so many robust babies: walking and eating shredded green papaya.

We walked through fields where lemongrass with slick, slender blades grew in tall bunches and smelled like sweet, fragrant spice. The fields led to forests, where eucalyptus trees stood, their trunks pale and bare and their leaves dancing like ruffles in the wind. The sky was endless. Dark clouds hung low.

"Don't wander off alone," Mom would say as she grabbed my hand, tightening her grasp around my knuckles. Some people in these parts had never seen white people before, she said, and if we didn't stay close they might want to take us away. I wondered what they wanted with plain old me, with my ugly brown hair and splotchy freckles and awkward knees. "Some people like to steal white kids and sell them for money," Mom told us.

■ ■

OUTSIDE THE WALLS, BESIDES THE dirt, Father David said there were evil spirits that would latch on to us like leeches if we weren't careful. He had his cartoonists draw up the invisible creatures so we'd know what they looked like: imps with spiny limbs, long fingers, sharp, curved fingernails, hunched backs, and devious smiles. Sometimes the evil spirits hid in humans, he said, "Like wolves in sheep's clothing." We had to be on guard at all times, not just for dirt and dangerous men that might like young girls, but for stealthy, unseen spirits that hid under the mask of a human face or a fake smile. That's why we stayed inside the walls, where it was clean and pure from evil and safe from the wolves. We were sheep, Father David said, being herded by God's good shepherd—him—into God's Heavenly Kingdom. And we were safe as long as we stayed within the walls of the compound.

Every time a member came home from being out in the dirt amid hosts of evil spirits and ignorant humans who may or may not be evil, depending on whether or not they wanted to hear our message, they changed clothes. They'd bathe thoroughly with Avery soap, which we had received as a donation. The soap was dyed an artificial forest green and, according to the English description of the Thai ingredients, was "rich with aloe vera" and "safe for all skin types." After scrubbing from head to toe, they'd change into clean clothes and indoor shoes and come inside to tell us testimonies of how many souls they'd saved that day for God's Heavenly Kingdom and how many miracles God performed by leading them to the right people, who gave them donations and free food. According to Thai custom, and because of the dirt and evil spirits, we never wore our street shoes in the house. Inside every home was a shoe rack stacked with rows of rubber flip-flops that had been marked with first and last initials. Mine said "FE" or had the symbol of the star accompanied by the number four. That was my new identity—"star four." I liked my new identity. I liked being a star.

CHAPTER 6

IN THE PICTURES FROM THE early days—Father David preaching at the Light Club at 116 Main Street in Huntington Beach, or gathering followers at the Texas ranch owned by Fred Jordan—Father David had his artists replace his head with that of a lion. I often wondered if I could peel away the whiteout to catch a glimpse of his face. He called himself MO Lion or King David or whatever name separated him from the rest of his flock and made him seem closer to God.

In the photos—which are dog-eared or stained or cracked down the middle—hippies gather in parks and on street corners, crowds of topless women hugging each other, bearded men holding Bibles and singing praises. Members formed colonies

in Europe, North and South America, Africa, and Southeast
Asia. The Children of God never stayed in one place for long.
Documentaries show grey footage of buses and caravans—the
sides painted with flowers and peace signs and Children of God
logos—moving at the orders of their leader, who never showed
his face. Father David saw the earth as a ticking time bomb, heading
toward demolition in 1993 when Armageddon would consume
the planet following the Great Tribulation, as told in the book of
Revelation. The members portrayed in the photos and film clips
were young. They were bold. They were revolutionaries, rebels who
owned minimal possessions and were attempting to create a world
modeled after the lyrics of John Lennon's "Imagine":

> Imagine no possessions,
> I wonder if you can.
> No need for greed or hunger,
> A brotherhood of man.

Father David required full dedication from his followers. It
was, as Dad put it, "no vacation." "Not for the faint of heart,"
Dad would say. His followers renounced all physical possessions
to be part of the Children of God in exchange for everlasting
rewards in heaven. Like a wildfire fueled by the followers' belief,
nothing could stop the new movement.

As the band of hippies grew to hundreds and then thousands, Father David formed layers of leadership. God was the
director. Jesus was the messenger. Father David was the interpreter. Mama Maria was his right-hand woman, who stood by
his side and recorded everything he said. A hierarchy of leaders
was appointed, which included National Area Shepherds (NAS),
General Area Shepherds (GAS), Home Shepherds (HS), and then
us, the soldiers in training.

Father David had a past most of his followers never knew about, or at least never cared to acknowledge. At age three, he was caught masturbating in church by his mother (he had been taught how by an older boy during a sermon) and was ordered to finish the act in front of his father. Both his parents were devout evangelists who'd been ostracized from the Disciples of Christ after his mother, Virginia Brandt, claimed a miraculous testament of "divine healing." She began preaching to crowds of thousands at the famed Miami Tabernacle about rising from her deathbed after an accident following the birth of her first son, Hjalmer. They joined the Christian and Missionary Alliance and took to the road as traveling evangelists. Father David came from a line of evangelists dating back two centuries. But he lived out a constant conflict between his sexual desire and his commitment to serving God.

As a young preacher, Father David claimed he had experienced sexual desire for his own mother in his early twenties while the two slept together in a hotel bed during one of their evangelical missions. He claimed there was nothing wrong with this desire. He said it was God's will that they sleep together, and it would have been sanctified had it not been for the stiff-mindedness of the "damn church." Soon he decided there needn't be such a struggle. "Anything done in the name of God is pure and good and should be celebrated and condoned" became a founding principle of the Children of God and the moral standard under which its children were raised. In Father David's new paradigm, sin was celebrated as a pathway to forgiveness, and guilt was abolished. His followers were sinners par excellence. Seeking to defy the tradition of the evangelical lineage he knew so well, Father David adopted his own belief system, which encouraged unconditional love and sexual freedom. He likened the traditional church to an "Old Wife"—stale and haggard—and called his new movement the "New Wife": young and sexy and full of life.

We all knew the story of Aaron, Father David's oldest son. Aaron was a talented musician who wrote songs and performed in California and around the United States. Wherever he played he gathered a crowd with his charming good looks. According to Father David's account, which he shared in his letters, one day Aaron had a calling to go back to his Heavenly Father, and he went to a mountaintop to heed the call. The image I had in my mind growing up was of a young man with golden locks and piercing blue eyes, a guitar strapped to his back, walking into puffy white clouds atop a high mountain in Switzerland. I imagined him a zealous follower of the voice of God, like Moses. Years later I discovered the truth: Aaron was driven to the brink of insanity by his father. He had left his young daughter to meet his fate by jumping off the cliff of a mountain. Father David's eldest son would be the first of many of his followers who would take their lives after serving for years in the Children of God.

CHAPTER 7

FOR TAMAR'S AND MY FIFTH birthday in Udon Thani, a friend of the Family whom we called Uncle Virgil gave each of us a fancy Mickey Mouse wristwatch. It had a purple band and gleaming silver trim, and Mickey's hands pointed to the appropriate numbers depending on what time it was. I wore that watch always, until one day Mickey's hands suddenly stopped ticking, and Mom told me we didn't have money to buy new lithium batteries.

Shortly after that birthday I began to obsess about death. Ever since I could remember, we'd been hearing about it. Our belief system centered around it. There was a predicted sequence of events that must occur before the Great Apocalypse, as told in the book of Revelation, translated by Father David, and transcribed by

Mama Maria. The Antichrist would rise to power and Father David would relay the news to us. The Antichrist would declare peace for seven years and announce a new world order. In the middle of his seven-year reign, he would break the contract and force everyone to receive the mark of the beast on their right hand or their forehead. Since members of the Children of God had been forewarned, we would refuse to receive the mark of the beast and would have to flee for our lives. Once we had exhausted all other hiding places, we would hide out in the mountains. The soldiers would raid our camp and send us to our deaths with machine guns and rifles and pistols.

It was our job to alert the whole world that the mark of the beast was a trap, and if people succumbed to the evil forces they would be selling their souls to the devil and would burn in hell for all eternity. Only those who received Jesus into their hearts as their Lord and Savior could go to heaven. Part of our role was to offer everyone salvation.

I turned five in December of 1986. Nineteen ninety-three seemed just around the corner. I did the math. I realized I would be twelve years old when the world ended. All the steps leading up to the Great Apocalypse would happen before then. I had seven years left to live.

■ ■

ONE NIGHT MOM TOLD US she was turning thirty-three. "The same age that Jesus was when he was crucified."

We were beside ourselves. Mary Ann was the first to start crying. She had a way of bursting into a fit of hysteria that made the rest of us follow suit. We were begging and pleading for God to not take Mom away. Mom told us not to worry.

"It doesn't mean that I am going to die," she said. "Jesus was a special person."

But that night I had a dream. I was run over by a motorcycle. The tires treaded through my organs, leaving me mangled, lying on the gravel and unable to move. My spirit left my body. I hovered over the pile of flesh and bones. I was completely aware that I was dead. Then I watched from the place above my physical body as a woman mounted the seat of the motorbike behind the male driver. Wrapping her arms around him, she tipped her helmet into position, ready for takeoff. She tilted her head back and allowed the breeze to tease her short black hair. She was definitely Asian, but I could not distinguish where she was from. Her skin was light and marked with blemishes. She didn't seem to notice that she had just been the cause of a tragic accident. I wasn't mad. I was happy to be liberated. She was happy too. Her face broke into a smile as the bike accelerated. They raced off, leaving me in my pile of mess, and I just watched. Instead of dread, anxiety, or even a palpable emptiness, I was just dead. Yet I felt strangely awake at the same time. There was a great aliveness accompanying my death. I was pure consciousness, roused by the release from my physical body.

I jolted awake, realizing it was a dream. My heart was racing. My palms were sweating. I patted my hands over parts of my body, feeling relieved that I was alive and still in my body. A part of me wanted to stay in that state, where I was fully awake forever.

■ ■

MOSTLY, I FEARED DEATH—DEEPLY. SOON began a series of sleepless nights, when I lay awake in my bed pondering how I was going to die. I prayed for the souls of those who were to kill me because I knew they weren't evil; they were just doing their jobs. Father David said we were God's martyrs. It was the price we had to pay for being God's chosen ones. Much of my childhood was spent fantasizing about the details of my death. I knew for sure I was going to heaven since I was one of God's children, but the threshold to get there seemed insurmountable.

Every night as I prepared for bed, I readied myself to awake at any moment to the surprise of men cloaked in black and carrying machine guns and rifles. But these men were human too. I thought that maybe I could convert them to our side. I convinced myself that if I could look into their eyes I could persuade them that I wasn't guilty of anything and that I didn't think they were bad either. They were soldiers like me. They didn't have a choice.

Life became a series of long, dark days followed by hot, restless nights. During the night, I imagined strong angels posted by my bedside to protect me, perhaps to make me invisible, or if nothing else to help me cope with the pain of the torture (because death was often preceded by torture). I slept close to the foot of Mom and Dad's bed whenever possible. That way I could position myself to slide under the bed at a moment's notice.

When a child is forced to think about death, they don't think about what will happen in the afterlife. They think about the exact moment of death and what must happen for a person to die. *Will it hurt? Will I be able to handle the pain? How will it happen? How long will it take?*

Most nights I prayed that I would just get shot. It seemed a quick and painless way. I wanted to be shot with a machine gun, making certain that I would die quickly, and I wanted to be shot in the heart. I was terrified of pistols and the idea of a wound that might leave me bleeding to death for hours.

One night Mom taped a verse to the wall by my bed: "All things work together for good to them that love God, to them that are called according to His purpose" (Romans 8:28). She also told me that God would never give me any temptation greater than I could bear.

I began to think about all the possible ways I could die, prim-itive ways that you hear about only from stories of the Middle Ages: being burned at the stake, crucified upside down, beheaded, or stoned to death. We were prepared for an invasion by the enemy, an army of men dressed in heavy black jumpsuits with helmets and batons and guns. I prayed, "Dear God, when they come to get me, make sure they aim right. I don't want to be shot in a place that will make me bleed to death. That would take too long. When they come to get me can You please make sure they shoot me right in the heart?" I located my heart in the left side of my chest. It was beating at an accelerated rate—thump, thump, thump—triggered by fear. I knew that if they got me in my chest it would be instant and certain, so that was my childhood wish—a gunshot to the heart.

"One more thing, God. If you want, you can take me in my sleep. I won't mind. Just help my mother cope with my death. Amen." On the nights when I was brave, I recited my own rendition of the timeless children's bedtime prayer:

Now I lay me down to sleep,
I pray the Lord my soul to take.
Please let me die before I wake,
I promise I won't make a peep.

Then I closed my eyes, a puddle of salty tears on my pillow, calmed my heart, thought about heaven, and fell to sleep.

CHAPTER 8

PREGNANT WOMEN WERE EVERYWHERE IN our compound. Auntie Vicky—not really our auntie—had a bulging belly and was ready to deliver any day. Pregnant moms were allowed to eat real milk and brown sugar and real eggs. They didn't have to eat boiled dal with whole tomatoes for breakfast or steamed hard tofu and steamed rice for lunch. Whenever a woman got pregnant she was put on a special protein-rich diet that included an extra-large portion of fish or some other protein if fish didn't agree with her. Mom had arranged for a doctor to come to the house to deliver Auntie Vicky's baby, but the morning Auntie Vicky's water broke the baby slipped right out. Mom wasn't qualified to deliver babies, but she played doctor and caught the baby as it came out. Tamar and I walked into the room to see Auntie Vicky on the bed with her legs spread open and her hair a mess, but still wearing her glasses. She didn't have time to take off her panties, which were stretched across her ankles.

I'd never seen a live birth, but I figured this was probably the closest I'd get. Later, Father David encouraged us kids to watch a delivery since we'd probably be having babies before too long. (Children who were members of the Family "came of age" young.)

Soon Mom was pregnant again, too. This would be child number seven, birth number eight. Our long walks took us by the hospital, and Mom cried silently at the prospect of giving birth in such a wretched place. Outside, on the lawn, we saw families huddled together waiting to hear news of their disabled loved one. In the maternity ward, twenty-some women shared the same room, with only a thin curtain separating one new mother from the next. Patients with open wounds lay close to babies freshly covered in vernix. With no other hospital within miles, Mom knew she had no choice but to deliver there. We didn't have money for a first-class hospital, so we learned to say we were missionaries, and the doctors delivered the baby for free.

Early one morning I was awakened to the sound of a rickety ambulance outside the walls. Mom's water had broken late in the night, and she had been rushed to the hospital. None of us knew she had left. We ran outside. The sky was turning grey. Dad helped Mom out of the ambulance and onto the dirt road. She wore her hospital gown with blue speckles and an open back. We hurried downstairs to meet our new baby sister. Dad told us to be careful and cautious.

"Usually new mothers stay in the hospital," Dad said. "But the doctor told Mom she could come home early because she could rest better here."

We climbed onto the couch and organized ourselves into

a neat row so we could take turns holding the baby. Dad went outside to fetch Mom and the newborn. The front door opened. Mom came in. Her legs were sturdy and strong, but the dimpled flesh on her knees sagged. Her eyes looked like she had just taken a long nap, and her hair was a tousled mess. Dad looked tired too.

Mom carried a tiny white bundle. She held the baby close, maybe as a gesture of gratefulness because the last one hadn't survived. Once she was inside I felt myself sink back into the couch. She walked slowly, each step a triumph. I froze. My breath deepened. I watched red fluid trickle slowly down the insides of her. Behind her on the polished wooden floor trailed footprints of blood, tiny pools that imitated the shape of her feet.

Later that evening we sat in a circle on Mom and Dad's bed to decide on the name of the baby. This was a ritual our family engaged in every time Mom brought a new one home. I chose "Rebecca Ann." "But we'll call her 'Becky,'" I said proudly. I was thrilled that I was old enough to participate in naming my new sister. It was even better than playing make-believe with my dolly. Becky was beautiful, with splotchy pink skin, blue eyes, and blond hair.

Until that day, I'd been obsessed with babies and having one of my own. Tamar and I would pretend to birth our dollies. I'd lie flat on my back and Tamar played nurse. I'd spread open my legs and "push," sliding the "baby" out from beneath my back. Tamar would catch it and slap it hard on its back to get it breathing. But after Mom's entrance that day, when I witnessed her exhaustion and her blood, I understood what was really involved in childbirth, and I decided I wanted to stay a child forever.

■ ■

I KNEW WHERE BABIES CAME from. It was commonplace to see the adults having sex in the homes we lived in—sometimes

within marriage, sometimes with other people's spouses; sometimes in the middle of the night in the cramped sleeping quarters,
and other times during broad daylight in a vacant bedroom. Father
David called it "sharing" and taught that it was selfish to hoard all
your love for one person.

Most of his followers didn't know that Father David had
become impotent shortly after founding the Children of God.
Still, so intent was he on advancing a sexual revolution that he
cheered on his members' sexual escapades and had young girls
send him videos of them dancing while wearing just a thin,
see-through scarf. He believed that sexual liberation should start
during childhood. That way kids wouldn't grow up with sexual
inhibitions and unhealthy attitudes toward God's beautiful act of
creation, he said.

Father David took the freedom to interpret the Bible as he
saw fit both in the early days and as his movement grew to thousands of followers. Sometimes visions came to him in his sleep,
and he'd wake up in a cold sweat. I can see him now, how his little
beady eyes stayed closed as he recalled and interpreted the dream,
while his faithful scribe, Mama Maria, grabbed the recording
device from the nearby nightstand. Everything had meaning, I
was taught. A dream was not a dream; it was a warning or a premo-
nition. A thought could come from God or the devil.

"Follow me and I will make you fishers of men" (Matthew
4:19). While interpreting that verse one day, Father David closed
his eyes and had a vision of an ocean. Inside the sea were lonely,
ugly fish. The fishermen were never interested in these fish
because they were unworthy of any purpose. He decided that the
fish represented the lonely, lost souls in desperate need of God's
love. The ocean was the world, and he and his followers were
fishermen, like Jesus and His disciples. Father David believed that
God's love was available to all those willing to receive it.

In the years before I was born, Father David sent his women followers out into the world to sell their bodies as a symbol of God's love; they would collect a generous "donation" in return for their services. Father David said that these women members were "bait." His letters instructed women to dress exotically, in sexy thigh-slit cocktail dresses, and to visit nightclubs and fancy hotel bars, where they'd spot lonely traveling men. They'd share a drink and enjoy a lovely slow dance then invite themselves to the men's hotel rooms. There they'd seduce them and tell them about God and his love. If the men had money, the women would request a donation. Father David taught the women how to recognize men with money by spotting their jewelry or fancy shoes. He said their accessories would be the dead giveaway even if the men were dressed casually or shabbily. Sometimes the men joined the Children of God; others left their hotels as newborn Christians and a little less lonely.

The practice was termed "flirty-fishing" because the women were trolling in the "dark ocean of the world." Father David considered flirty-fishing to be an act of martyrdom—women sacrificing their bodies in the name of God's love. He called the women "hookers for Jesus." The men targeted for flirty-fishing were labeled "beasts"—the lonely, the unattractive, the impotent. Many children born within the movement in the seventies were conceived through flirty-fishing. Father David called them Jesus Babies since Jesus was an illegitimate child too, sown in the womb of his mother by the archangel Gabriel. Flirty-fishing was banned in 1987, when I was five, soon after the AIDS epidemic became rampant.

Despite his own incapacity, Father David didn't shy away from his sexual desire and need for expression. In his top-secret hideout he kept his collection of videos of scarf-clad young girls dancing to a hot Hawaiian number. (I knew this because he sent out letters talking about his active sex life *and* I'd seen the videos.)

I was never required to dance on tape for him, but by the time I was seven I already knew in detail from his letters what it took to please a woman and the best way to get a man off, although I was more schooled in the "pleasing the woman" part since that was supposedly Father David's forte. The most beautiful thing in creation, he believed, was a woman, with her lovely curves and "mountainous abodes'" as he described female breasts. A tree came in a close second, with its strong roots and heavenly branches reaching up like arms outstretched to the sky.

In the early days of the movement, children as young as eight years old in his home were encouraged to take part with each other in what Father David called "love-up" time. This would happen after morning devotions and to Father David was part of the daily routine, as natural as eating and breathing. Adult-child sex was banned, but not until 1986, and I was never forced to participate.

One of my first and sharpest memories is from my early years in California. I'm walking on a cement driveway, and the particles of concrete seem to jump up at me as if they're alive. For a moment, I'm transported to another world. I feel myself merge with the pulsating ground as the granules metamorphose into a bubbly arrangement. I regain my focus and shake myself back into consciousness. I'm only three years old and I'm wondering why I'm here and why I'm me. The yellow and orange curtains on the left side of the house are closed shut, and there is no way for anyone to see inside. Some young teens have been put on duty to watch over us smaller children. I am fully aware that all the adults are inside engaging in a sexual congregation. I don't know how I know, but I'm certain an orgy is taking place inside—while I walk around outside questioning my existence on Earth.

Voyeuristic displays of adult affection became daily routine. Sometimes the adults knew we were watching; sometimes our own curiosity led us to investigate. Soon I found myself engrossed in them. In Udon Thani, one morning during breakfast, Auntie Ecclesia came downstairs to the breakfast table, threw her arms around Uncle Simon, and gave him the biggest hug, the kind reserved for adults only. She wrapped one leg around his waist, and pulled herself closer so their pelvises were pressed tightly together. They started praising the Lord and thanking Jesus for his love, and we all knew what that meant: they had spent most of the night doing something other than sleeping.

Most nights we kids stayed in a room upstairs with our parents. A divider separated Mom and Dad's bed from the rest of us. On one side of the divider was a mirror Dad covered up because Tamar and I were becoming "too vain," he told us. "Every time you look in the mirror you become uglier and uglier," he said. Dad never raised his voice, so even when he reprimanded us I didn't mind a bit. I knew he had a duty to correct me.

When no one was looking, I pulled aside the wrinkled pastel-green sheet and took a peek. Just to make sure I was still cute. Just to make sure I wasn't ugly. But never, *ever* did I wish to be beautiful, because beauty meant desire and desire meant sex, and since I was a chosen child of God I knew I would be required to share God's love when I came of age—something I didn't want to do.

CHAPTER 9

THE LEADERSHIP ESTABLISHED A SCHOOL in Japan called the Heavenly City School (HCS). It was the flagship home, and it housed up to three hundred members. It was large and spacious with multiple houses, and was surrounded by acres of grassy hills and Japanese gardens on a lot that spanned a whole block. I was jealous of the lucky kids who ended up there. A wealthy Japanese sponsor had donated it to the Family. The Children of God had now grown to twelve thousand members, the children far outnumbering the adults.

The HCS was equipped with a studio, where members produced tapes, posters, and videos for distribution. Flirty-fishing and other controversial methods of outreach from the early days had been banned after bad publicity from the press and because of the recent discovery of AIDS in 1981. Now the Family made money by having its members give away the media (called "tools") for a suggested donation. We also had sponsors who donated money and supplies, so we always lived in beautiful houses with affordable rent that had large yards and high walls, two requirements that had to be kept in mind whenever members went "house hunting." We never knew how long a home would be available before neighbors or landlords became suspicious of our unusual living arrangements and we'd have to pack up and find a new place.

In order to carry out Father David's method of converting the world one heart at a time, we were ordered by the leadership to go on "witnessing trips." The adults who were assigned to travel were usually fun and adventurous, not strict and vigilant like our home shepherds. Sometimes we kids participated, even though we weren't solely responsible for making money. It was the only time we got to leave the compound. I liked the days when I didn't have to sit and listen to God's word for hours and instead went witnessing in unfamiliar cities or rural towns. For every soul we won, we received an extra star on our crown in heaven. I thought of my heavenly crown, bright and shiny and full of stars.

Mom didn't go outside the compound much since she was usually pregnant, but Dad quickly learned to speak Thai almost fluently and was soon able to get by with the locals with little to no translation. I was starting to gather that their commitment was to the group more than to us kids, and deep inside I missed my family terribly. Even though we all lived under the same roof, things were different here from the way they were in California. When we went witnessing we traveled by *tuk-tuk, song taow,* or taxi. Some were day trips; others lasted three to five days. They were scheduled productions organized by a home shepherd. After we had hit up every local business and knocked on every door in proximity to our home, asking residents and business owners if they'd like to invite Jesus into their hearts as their Lord and Savior to guarantee them a spot in heaven come the Great Apocalypse in 1993, we'd expand our radius by spending a few days in parts more rural than Udon Thani—villages only accessible by dirt road or motorbike.

We braved the dirt. Sometimes the men rode bicycles. Or we tackled public transportation—crowded buses that stayed in one spot for what seemed like hours. I would take a nap and wake up an hour later and we'd still be in the same spot as when I fell asleep, surrounded by sweaty bodies and the aroma of humid street pollution and deep-fried chicken from the roadside vendors. The dirt had a way of seeping into the open-air buses, settling on plastic seat covers and on the black steering wheel and making it difficult to breathe.

After we got to our destination, we found hotels to stay in for free. Fluffy dirt feathered the ceiling fan blades, filmed the walls in a sticky grime, and curtained the thin screen windows that were installed near the ceiling for ventilation. Dirt latched onto cobwebs and collected in floor corners. Whenever we turned the fans on (there was no air conditioning in third-class hotels), they showered us with puffs of dirt curdles, and I had to keep my mouth closed to prevent the dirt from coating my teeth and gums.

We spent our time in regions where people had never heard of God or the Family—Chiang Rai, Koh Samui, or some remote island or village where roads became bumpy dirt paths. Some residents of these far-flung destinations had never seen white people, as Mom had pointed out on our long afternoon walks to the eucalyptus fields in Udon Thani. We kept a detailed log of everywhere we went, along with a tally of souls won. We didn't want to hit the same place twice or raise unnecessary suspicions about why young kids were out for hours a day and not in school. We'd witness to as many people as we could and pray with them to ask Jesus into their hearts. "Win as many souls as possible for God's Heavenly Kingdom," Father David commanded.

I'd been living in Udon Thani six months when I went on my first witnessing trip, an excursion to a rural village, where I met a woman who could not stop hiccupping. Our encounter with her stuck in my mind for that reason and others. Mom and Uncle Simon were with me. The woman was pregnant and ran a dry-cleaning business along with her husband on the side of a dirt road in a town whose name I'll never remember. She invited us into her shop. As we stepped through the glass doors, the air conditioner hummed around us. It was cool inside and we were safe from the dirt. She wore a shirt patterned with pastel pink flowers that had pointed petals and green leaves. It was made of a flimsy polyester material and had a loose collar and sleeves that went to the middle of her arms. Her stomach bulged. She told us that her husband beat her. She had no protection against him because with one hand she covered her mouth to excuse the incessant hiccups and with the other she held her belly.

Behind the woman, racks of clothing wrapped in crisp plastic coverings trudged along on conveyor belts. In one corner sat a fat porcelain Buddha, goofy-grinned and cross-legged with his hands in his lap. Father David had warned us about heathen statues. He said they were like the golden cow the Israelites fashioned when Moses was in the mountains receiving the Ten Commandments from God. Along with evil spirits, ignorant humans, dangerous men, and dirt, we had to also be on guard for statues of idols and insincere worship. My instincts were at an all-time high. I learned to spot a white Buddha statue or a tangerine-robed monk from a mile away.

I observed other items in the shop. There was the traditional portrait of the king and queen with fruit and flowers and incense and little crumpled pieces of paper with prayers written on them underneath the altar shrine. A table in the corner had a rice cooker ready with steamed rice, and a pot on the stove bubbled with soup that smelled of lemongrass and fish. The odors of spices and steamed vegetables combined to make a sweet fragrance. The shop had bamboo floors. We took off our shoes and walked barefoot on the smooth wooden planks.

The woman's husband wasn't there. She offered us Thai sweets that tasted of coconut and cane sugar. They were gooey and dripped with coconut oil. I savored those sweets, *ka nom,* because it was rare that I could eat something made from real sugar and oozing with coconut fat. We didn't have money to buy sugar or any kind of fat, which was considered a luxury. I was happy to be out of the home, exploring the streets of the city and eating real Thai food and delicious desserts and not having to listen to God's word or confess my sins.

Back when we busked on the streets in California or in the shopping mall in front of JCPenney, I didn't care much about the person we were witnessing to. Although most adults, including my parents, were excited about the task, witnessing had become routine and something that was required of me, but never something I wanted to do or felt compelled to do. I was shy, and even at a young age I found it humiliating to tell people about Jesus and beg them for money. Most of my siblings, including Mary Ann and Tamar, shared in my apprehension, but John was known to at least act enthusiastic about the task. He learned to speak Thai better than the rest of us. This woman was different from the people I had encountered in California—I couldn't keep my eyes off her. Her hair was tied back in a half-ponytail and her arms were plump and firm. She spoke English brokenly. Her words came out disjointed, so we had to piece them together.

"Yoo come in syde," she said. She gestured to us, one hand leading the way to a glass table and chairs and the other hand covering her mouth as she hiccupped relentlessly and uncontrollably.

Usually Mom got busy asking people if they wanted to hear about Jesus, but Mom also had a way of listening to people that I admired. And if the person who was talking had a stomach bulging with a baby, she listened more intently. As the mother of seven living children and one dead baby, that was her way of connecting with other mothers.

In between the woman's words were gaps of hiccups. She covered her mouth with one hand and with the other rubbed her belly or placed it on her tired hip. Her eyes were drained and her face weary. Her hiccups were spaced about ten seconds apart. "I never stop," she said. And then she gulped a hiccup that made her round belly jump. "Ever since I go pregnant, and the doctor he no know what the matter."

I could tell that Mom listened because she cared, not just because Father David said that God required compassion of all His children. She sucked in gasps of "*Jah!*" that I knew were indicative of her Swedish heritage and that came out when she was listening attentively. Perhaps this woman was being heard for the first time in her life.

"My family they no like my husband," she said. "He not nice to me."

She rubbed her belly and looked down. In the course of a minute, ten hiccups gulped through her throat and made her whole body jump. She was sad and she was in pain and it wasn't just because of the hiccups or her swollen belly.

After a while her husband came home. We had learned how to discern by a person's demeanor whether or not they were receptive to our message of Jesus and God's love and the looming Rapture, and this man wasn't. He came in angry and he talked in loud Thai, commanding his wife to do this and do that, ordering her around like a shepherd herding sheep. His anger wouldn't be calmed. We weren't to force our message on others if they weren't receptive. So we said goodbye in Thai and walked out the store and on to the next door.

Hours later we passed by the dry cleaner's. I saw the woman sitting in her chair with her belly on her lap. Her husband was shouting at her with his hands in the air. He appeared ready to hit her. Her head hung low. With one hand she held her mouth to excuse her hiccups. With her other she held her belly.

Looking back now, I realize that this memory stuck in my mind because it was the first time I had encountered someone outside the group and realized that she was no different than me. I had been taught that everyone outside the group was either lost or evil, but this woman was neither evil nor lost; she was a woman in pain. On a deep, visceral level, I was experiencing empathy for a person who was not part of the Family. This woman wasn't evil, nor did she need my help. She was just a woman in a shop and we met for a brief moment and I would probably never meet her again. At the time, I was too young to question my beliefs based on that encounter, but I knew that my feelings were valid and true and reflected an awareness that I wasn't allowed to acknowledge growing up.

My shoes kicked up dust as we walked past the store.

■ ■

AFTER A DAY OF WITNESSING, we provisioned a meal of street food—crunchy, deep-fried chicken dripping with hot grease, sticky rice with papaya salad and sweet vinegar dressing. We carried the food, wrapped in oily paper bags, to our hotel room. We showered in the bathroom, using a plastic dipper to splash cold water all over our bodies where the dirt hid. We ate our dinner with our hands, using the greasy paper bags as plates.

From a young age I developed compulsive behaviors that became very apparent on our witnessing trips. It started when I lost my first tooth and refused to let anyone pull it out. I let it stay loose in my gums until it rotted and turned blue and purple and fell out on its own. I was obsessed with my bangs and fussed if they were out of place or fell flat on my forehead. I started sucking on the tips of my hair and peeling the skin from my cuticles until they swelled with pus and bled. Nighttime was the worst. I was so scared that I would lie in bed shivering until I cried myself to sleep. Soon my pillow became my comfort. I was particular about its degree of firmness. When I was out witnessing, the thing I missed most was my pillow. I couldn't fall asleep without it.

I asked Mom if I could call home from a telephone booth to talk to Dad. I also missed him terribly. I went outside with Mom and dropped the coin in the slot and dialed the number. It had started raining in the late afternoon, and now the rain was coming down in sheets. The glass booth shielded me. Dad answered.

"How's it going, babes?" he asked. "Fine," I whimpered. The receiver was filthy and I knew there were invisible germs so I was careful not to touch my mouth to it. Father David warned against germs like they were accomplices of the Devil. Diseases were a spiritual invasion that we must guard against at all times lest we become contaminated with sickness or worse. I strained to hear my father's voice above the patter of rain drops against the glass.

"How's the pillow at the hotel?" he asked. Dad knew I was particular about my pillow. He knew I liked my hair a certain way and that I would get fussy if my bangs were out of place. He didn't know I was also worried about death and the end of the world, because I kept those fears to myself.

"It's okay," I admitted. My pillow at home was firm.

I fiddled with the curly phone wire and gripped the metal holder. I started to cry.

"I miss my pillow," I managed between sobs of tears. Sheets of warm rain were pouring against the glass. The hotel pillows were packed with a soft, downy filling that felt like feathers but was probably just an imitation of feathers since the hotels we stayed in were third-class hotels and were free, not expensive first-class resorts like I'd seen on the islands and on postcards. When I slept on the hotel pillows they made my neck sore.

"The hotel pillows are too soft," I said. "They're not firm like my pillow at home. And I miss it. I can't sleep well without my pillow, Daddy."

"Next time, babes, you can bring your pillow," Dad said. "Okay? I promise. I'll pack it up for you before you leave."

I wanted to tell Dad I missed him too, but I couldn't get the words out.

CHAPTER 10

EARLY ONE MORNING AFTER WE'D been living in Udon Thani nearly three months, Dad strapped a money belt around his waist. It was old and dark beige with small metal buckles. Inside he kept nine passports and a small ration of money that would get us across the border and back. Wherever we lived, Dad was the financial manager for the home and kept a detailed log of money coming in and money going out. He had a knack for math and the sciences. He said the only problem was there wasn't much money to keep track of, so his job was "easy as pie."

When we lived in Thailand, I looked forward to the days when we woke up before dawn. It meant ninety long days had passed and it was time to travel out of the country to renew our visas. I kept a chart on the wall next to my bed and marked off the days between visa trips. On the nights when I didn't stay up crying, dreading the thought of my own predetermined death, I spent the hours in anticipation, counting the days until I could be alone with my immediate family for legal purposes.

Mom woke us up early. On the breakfast table were real fried eggs, rice, and peanut butter sandwiches with bright-colored jam on fluffy white bread. Mom told us to make sure to pee even if we didn't have to so we wouldn't have to use the public restrooms on the train or at the station because they were unsanitary and polluted.

At the train station Dad got busy doing paperwork and Mom told us to be well-behaved and to act "normal." The train would only take us so far, stopping short of the Malaysian border. There we would pass through customs. "I'm a teacher," Dad would tell the border patrol officers in Thai. "I teach English to the military." We tried all sorts of facades: Dad was a teacher; John was adopted; we were here on vacation. But never, ever could we make it known who we really were: missionaries on a quest to save the world from the Great Apocalypse. Father David said never were we allowed to witness to any person in uniform. We knew how to recognize an undercover officer by their choice of shoes, which were always polished and black no matter how grungy they dressed. I was prepared to run. We stuck close together. John counted to manage his nervousness, and we would laugh and imitate him with his worried face, his unease characteristic of his anxious firstborn's personality.

We wore matching clothes. The night before, a Filipina auntie styled my and my sisters' hair into tight French braids that turned our eyes slanty and our scalps bright red. We left the braids in for days, taking them out only once the fuzzy flyaway escapees became unmanageable. For that one day, one of my wishes was granted: my hair was curly. But I was still tall, and I still didn't know how I was going to die. (My two wishes as a child were to be short with curly hair, and to have a quick, painless death.)

The Thai people loved to touch us. As we walked through the markets, hands reached out from the dark and grabbed our arms and touched our skin like we were celebrities. People stopped us in the middle of the street and peeled oranges, carefully stripping away the white veiny fibers, and fed us the juicy slices. They made a big deal over us. They kissed us and took pictures and counted us. They would *Ohhh* and *Ahhh* over such a rare sighting as a large family of white children, comparing us to the von Trapps from *The Sound of Music*. Mom held Becky close. She didn't want her to be contaminated by the filth of the streets. After people touched us Mom passed around the bottle of disinfectant she carried in her purse, pouring it all over our hands, telling us to rub our faces and arms thoroughly. She told us to watch our things.

"Sometimes people like to smuggle drugs over with innocent white kids," Mom said. I looked into the distance. Beyond the train tracks and the dirt road, I saw a picture of a rope looped into a circle the size of a hefty neck. I knew what that meant: smuggling drugs was punishable to death by hanging. I was scared of being hanged in the End Time. I didn't know what made me eligible for such a primitive death, except for being God's child. Father David made sure we knew stories about criminals who were hanged for murder, and tales of martyred saints, like Peter, Jesus's disciple who was hanged upside down on the cross. He told us these stories to prepare us for our future fate. I knew only about archaic ways of dying. I didn't know about things like lethal injection or nuclear bombs that could kill people in an instant with little to no pain.

On the trains, we whizzed by rice paddies and through slums where nothing existed but miles and miles of shacks that zoomed by so fast they looked like one long, blurry, wooden house.

Mom gave us each a carton of chocolate milk for every train ride. We savored the thick, sweet concoction and attempted to stretch our indulgent allowance for as long as we possibly could. We never ate or drank anything containing sugar except on visa trips, when we were allowed to so we could look as normal as possible, Mom said. At home, we didn't have sugar aside from the rotten bananas, boiled molasses, and huge blocks of raw cane sugar that we kept for special occasions. We invented a game that forced us to make our treat last: we would take a sip only while we were zooming across a bridge. We waited in anticipation, our mouths watering for more, and gulped cautiously as we crossed between the zigzag bars that prevented the train from tipping into the milky brown water below. We traveled down the strip of land that resembled an elephant's trunk, usually sleeping on the train overnight, tossing and swaying in the rumble of third-class comfort.

Tamar and I shared a bunk and always whined for the top. We usually managed to get our way since we were twins and had a majority vote. We invented a game called tickle-scratch that helped us relax and fall right to sleep. We were the perfect match for each other, our bodies fitting together as we positioned ourselves to lay with our heads on opposite ends, our identical white feet resting near the other's head. One was assigned to be "Tickle," the other "Scratch." We alternated assignments appropriately. Tickle first. We would tease the skin of each other's feet with soft, circular motions using our nails and the tips of our fingers. Once we couldn't bear the tingly sensation anymore and wanted to jolt our legs away, Scratch would call out, "Scratch!" We scratched vigorously until the bottoms of our feet turned red. Then the other commanded, "Tickle!" The process continued until we passed out from exhaustion and fell asleep near each other's feet, Tamar's one size bigger than mine since she was nineteen minutes older than me.

I loved those train rides because I knew there was no way possible that the Antichrist could arise to power on such short notice and make it on to the train to capture me there. As long as we were moving and I felt the rumble of the train tracks beneath me, I knew I was safe—my life extended for one more day.

After getting off the train Dad hailed a taxi to take us to the ferry into Malaysia. It took him an extra-long time since he had to find a vehicle big enough to fit him, Mom, and us seven kids. Usually he'd settle for a Chevrolet.

"Chev-vee tao alli?" he would ask—"How much for the Chevy?" Once a fare was agreed to, he sat in the front passenger's seat, which was on the left side. We kids piled into the back of the banana-colored vehicle, dressed in matching uniforms and chewing gum with earnest intention, savoring every burst of sugary, minty sweetness. All the taxi drivers had extra-dark skin. Their nails were short and lined with dirt, except for one pinky nail, which they kept long to pick their nose or snort cocaine, we later gathered.

When we reached the Malaysian border, Dad did extensive paperwork while Mom watched us kids play house in the flower beds and snack on peanuts and raisins or exotic fruits such as longans or rambutans. We had to pay ten baht to use the bathroom. The toilet was a hole in the floor that you had to flush with buckets of water. I wondered who the guy accepting the coins was and if he was hired or if he was just taking our money because we were foreigners and if you're white you're supposed to have money. But we were just as poor as the guy taking the money at the squat-toilet. The only difference was we had a reason to be poor. We were broke with a cause: we were saving the world.

CHAPTER 11

FATHER DAVID MADE IT CLEAR we weren't to witness to our neighbors. He didn't want us to raise a suspicion about our living conditions; nor did he want them calling the authorities if they became wary. We left the house in shifts and never had more than eight or ten people in the yard at one time. When we were outside, we made sure to look like we were doing something productive, like raking leaves, mowing the lawn, or painting the wooden fence. When we saw neighbors through the gates or workmen peering over the walls, we learned to duck out of view by disappearing behind bushes or trees.

We routinely staged imitation raids. The adults dressed up like soldiers, wearing helmets and all-black clothing and carrying mock batons and broomsticks for guns. Close to bedtime, they banged on the front doors and then burst through them. We hid under the stairs. They pretended to kill us with their broomstick guns, and we responded by falling to the floor and pretending to die, lying still and silent, and then rising in ecstasy to heaven, a place of "no more tears." In a state of near euphoria, we sang songs about heaven, raising our arms in the air and pantomiming flying up to heaven to meet Jesus at the pearly gates. I raised my arms, although I was never euphoric. How did nobody understand that I was terrified about what needed to happen in order for us to get to heaven? Did they not understand that death comes before resurrection?

■ ■

WE KNEW IT WAS ONLY a matter of time before someone found us—thirty to fifty foreigners crammed in houses in the boonies of Thailand, none of us speaking a single word of Thai except for traditional phrases: *Sawadee ka* ("Hello") or *Kop khun ka* ("Thank you"). I also knew how to pray with someone to ask Jesus into his or her heart, fluently.

Father David taught us to be prepared for the kind of invasion that might be triggered by the suspicion of meddlesome neighbors. He sent out a letter urging each member to have a "flee bag" packed with basic necessities—shirts, socks, underwear, a few toiletries—in case we had to run away quickly in the middle of the night. We called it preparing for "evacuation."

I had heard stories about evacuations. A home in Argentina called a "Jumbo" had housed up to three hundred members. It was raided by officials during the wee hours. After being interrupted from their sleep and snatched out of bed, the children were ordered by officials to board a bus and were taken to social services, where they remained until their parents were proven innocent of child abuse and molestation charges. We were taught how to answer questions properly so authorities wouldn't think we were abused or "too sheltered."

"Did you grow up in a sect?" our uncles, aunties, and shepherds probed us after we emerged from hiding under the stairs during an imitation raid.

"What's a sect?" we'd answer after being drilled to say so in unison and on queue.

"Have you been brainwashed?" they prodded. Sometimes they quizzed us as a group, sometimes one by one.

"There's no such thing as brainwashing," we answered, in either a timid response or a thunderous roar of disingenuous affirmation.

I wondered why we had to pretend we were doing nothing wrong if we really weren't and why we had to pretend to be honest if we really were. At a young age I began to question if there really was such a thing as brainwashing. The cover-up and all the questions just didn't make sense to me.

We were told that when the Jumbos was raided, the children were interrogated into exhaustion. The girls were taken to the doctor to be examined so it could be determined whether they were still virgins, a procedure, described to us graphically, that involved a cold speculum and metal foot stirrups. Although I was horrified by that notion, I secretly wondered what it would be like to be my own version of Annie and live in a stable home with rich parents, even if only temporarily. Guiltily, I wondered what it would be like to be an only child and have parents who could give me everything I wanted and to live in a fancy house with high glass cupboards filled with delicate china sets.

■ ■

ONE DAY DURING BREAKFAST UNCLE Jeremiah made an announcement. "It looks like Joy's mother is after us," he said. "She wants to take me to court to get the kids."

Joy was Uncle Jeremiah's daughter. She lived with us in Udon Thani. She had long, sleek hair that fell well below her waist. She was thirteen, which to me meant she was an adult. Joy's mother had left the Family. Father David called the people who left "backsliders." "Damn backsliders," he'd say. "Looking to disrupt God's mission."

I knew this was common in the Family. The parent who left would return to try to take back their children. Sometimes the episodes turned into messy court battles. Sometimes the backslider parent would use force—breaking in, kidnapping. Since we lived mostly in third-world countries that lacked solid social-services systems, the parent would barge into the home in the middle of the night with police officers in tow. When these kinds of invasions happen in America nowadays, they make headline news, but back then no one had heard of such events, especially in places like Argentina or the Philippines.

I wanted Joy to stay. She was pretty. She had dark, mysterious eyes, and everyone said she was exotic, with her jet-black hair. I knew what Uncle Jeremiah's announcement meant—that we would have to be on our toes, ready for an invasion in the middle of the night. It was exciting and exhilarating. But it was also terrifying. I realize now that terror was home to me. It was all I knew. There was magic in the mystery of the unknown. Pretty soon I wouldn't know how to function without the drama of trepidation. Fear had become my closest friend, my ally. Fear would become a tool I would learn to wield in order to operate in the world, even much later in life.

And then it did happen. Early one morning I awoke to the untimely flash of fluorescent lights and mother's urgent command. "Hurry and get your things together. We have ten minutes to pack and vacate." She told us to be as quiet as possible. Outside, the sky was still dark. Mattresses covered with baby-blue sheets were stretched across the floor. "Hurry, kids! Before the officials get here." Her voice was pressing but calm. Mom knew how to remain tranquil and composed during emergency situations, probably because giving birth isn't the most relaxing procedure, and she'd already done that eight times and was still as robust as ever, even though one of them came out dead.

Mary Ann was rubbing her eyes, and John was helping Dad pack our things. Tamar and I got dressed quickly and ran downstairs, where Mom was getting William and Heidi ready.

"Where are we going?" Mary Ann, who had just come downstairs, asked.

"We don't know," Dad said. "We just have to leave now!" Becky was sleeping in her bassinet. We had been at Udon Thani for six months—the longest I'd ever lived in a home.

"It's time to say good-bye," Mom said. "We don't have much time." I was used to saying good-bye, but this time I was saying good-bye to my childhood, even though I was only five years old. I was saying good-bye to just one of many houses we would vacate over the years. We were always fleeing from something, it seemed: first America, now the officials. This time they were coming to take away Joy, who had slept on the floor on a mattress next to my bed.

Nothing much else was said. Whenever we were ordered to do something we simply listened and obeyed. That was the way. There were no questions. We lived every day on the verge of martyrdom and thankful for each day as another privilege, another chance to save the world.

A *song taow* was waiting for us outside the gates. We positioned ourselves to fit into the open-air vehicle, accompanied by our most important possessions stuffed into large black trash bags. The air was cool and the sky was lifting from dark to grey. If Dad was worried he never showed it.

Mom was holding Becky, still a newborn, in her arms. She looked at Dad, who was loading the last of our belongings.

"Are they all here?" She began to count us the way she did when she didn't have a free hand, using her head to nod off the numbers one by one.

"One. . . two. . . . Where's William?"

William was sitting behind Heidi with her fire-red hair, sucking on her pacifier.

"Three. . . four. . . ." We twins always stuck together.

"Five. . . six. . . seven." Becky was cradled in her arms.

John followed suit in his worried way, as he always did whenever we were out in public, just to double-check, just to be the big brother that he was.

"One. . . "—counting himself—"two. . . three. . . four. . . five. . . six. . . seven."

We were all present and quiet, no one uttering a word.

I didn't ask where we were going. I knew we had no destination. We were fleeing and I was thrilled and anxious by the idea of it. I lived my life prepared to flee. I had my flee bag close by, packed with the basic necessities for survival. In case a natural disaster hit or the Antichrist rose to power, I was ready to escape at the snap of a finger, just like we had to that morning, when they came to take Joy. We all, including Joy and her family, had escaped.

We drove off into the early morning hours, leaving behind a trail of dust and memories of the house near the banks of the Mekong River.

CHAPTER 12

THE DIRT ROADS WERE BUMPY and wound through bright green meadows. I held my dolly close so she wouldn't get startled by the rough ride. The driver swerved suddenly and randomly. Tamar was holding her dolly close too.

"Look." Tamar pointed to sharp blades of grass that grew taller than the top of Dad's head. The sides of the roads fell away into swamps. "If we're not careful we could fall right in."

Piles of garbage in the villages gave off a sour stench that lasted in my nose for days. Sickly and scrawny dogs emerged from the piles of rotting trash that swarmed with flies. They barely looked like dogs but instead like oversized rats with patchy fur and open, bloody wounds. Sometimes they hobbled on just two or three legs.

Dad had made a lot of calls from a pay phone near the edge of Udon Thani, finally finding us a new home that had room for our big family. We were going to a city called Khorat, in the central part of Thailand. (A home in Chiang Mai, near the Burmese border, part of the northernmost region of the country known for its lush, mountainous rainforests and historic sacred temples, was taking in the rest of the members we'd been living with.) Our drive took the rest of the day, and when we arrived at our new home the sky was fading to grey. A few adult members came out to greet us.

"Hi, I'm Auntie Joan." A woman walked briskly toward us, beaming. She wore no makeup but was pretty in a plain way. "I'm one of the home shepherds. And this here is Uncle Josh."

Uncle Josh was smiling too. He had curly hair, muscular arms, and dark skin, and he wore an apron with no shirt. His tan made him look like he had just come from one of the nearby tropical islands. Uncle Josh and Auntie Joan praised the Lord and thanked Jesus. They greeted us like we were family. I wanted to feel that we had arrived home, but I felt strangely alone.

"Kids, say hi," Mom prodded. Tamar grabbed my hand.

"Oh, thank the Lord," Auntie Joan said. "God will always lead his children to safety."

As Auntie Joan led us inside we saw a trail of dark drops on the pavement leading to the front door. Heidi bent down to touch one, and John pulled her back.

"What's that?" Mary Ann asked. "Is that blood?"

Another girl in the home had stepped on a nail the night before. The droplets made a path from the garage, where she must've gashed her foot, to the front door. Auntie Joan told us they'd had to take her to the hospital, which is how we knew it must have been an emergency. We never went to the hospital except in cases of severe emergency, like the time Becky split open her lip and had to get stitches. Doctors were phonies, Father David said, and besides, since we were dying and going to heaven soon, there was no need to preserve our physical bodies on earth.

Auntie Joan showed us into a small room to shower and change for dinner. There were a few beds, a dresser against the wall, and a small wood-frame window in the corner. The last rays of light shone through thin white curtains.

"What a beautiful family! God has surely blessed you." Auntie Joan glanced around at us kids as if she were counting us. "You will be a *wonderful* addition to our home. Hallelujah."

Uncle Josh, the home cook, said dinner would be held in the dining room at six o'clock sharp. "Do you kids like fish? The Lord provided! I can't keep up with the supply. Hallelujah. Fish for breakfast. Fish for lunch. And fish for dinner. Jesus is working miracles." I noticed that every sentence in our new home seemed punctuated with praise for the Lord.

As we got ready for dinner, we heard a sound coming from an upstairs bathroom window. It was the sound of a child's screams as he was being beaten—incessantly, slowly, and rhythmically. I felt Tamar's hand grip tighter around mine. We reasoned we'd have to be very good in our new home to avoid both punishment from the adults and punishment from God, which was the reason we found for why that girl had injured her foot so badly. She must've done something bad for God to punish her.

The noise of the screaming child seemed to go on for hours.

■ ■

THE KHORAT HOME WAS MUCH bigger than our house in Udon Thani. The dining hall fit thirty to forty people easily. There were rows of tables with adjoining wooden benches, much like the picnic benches I remembered from the campgrounds of California. Groups began filing in. People, it seemed, were everywhere. The swarm of introductions made me dizzy.

"Since it's your first night here, you're welcome to spend dinner together as a family," Auntie Joan said, smiling, as she greeted us in the dining hall. She led us to a small wooden table with benches and two chairs. It was a tight squeeze, but we managed to fit all seven of us, plus Mom and Dad. It was clear from Auntie Joan's words that beginning the next day, we would be separated.

Before eating, everyone chanted a prayer together, and then a woman read some news from Father David and welcomed us. This woman also said "Hallelujah," "Praise the Lord," and "Thank you, Jesus" a lot. From the way she announced our arrival, I got the sense that sudden, unexpected moves like ours were not uncommon. We were just one family passing through and were not expected to stay long. I hoped so; I wanted to be in a smaller home again or maybe even alone with my family.

Auntie Joan said we could sleep in a room with our parents for the night; the next morning we would be divided into groups according to age. John would be with the older kids; Mary Ann, Tamar, and I would be with a few other kids our age; and William and Heidi would be in another group. Becky could stay with Mom for most of the day since she was still breast-feeding, but soon she'd have to go to a group designated for babies. I was happy that at least I would be in a group with Tamar and Mary Ann.

Auntie Joan pressed her hands on her knees and bent down to meet our gaze. "You're going to love your new friends," she said. "They're much more than friends. They're your family in the Lord." She smoothed her hand through my hair, and I got a queasy feeling in my stomach.

■ ■

WHEN I AWOKE THE NEXT morning the sharp light from the windows gave me a splitting headache. The sun was blinding and much brighter than in the mountainous province of Udon Thani, where clouds lingered even without rain. I felt disoriented and confused.

"It's time to go to your new groups," Mom said. "Let's all be good, happy children." I didn't want to go, but I didn't want to make a fuss either.

It wasn't just being separated from Mom and Dad that was difficult. It was also seeing my younger siblings being torn apart from our parents. William and Heidi started wailing for Mom, who still had Becky in her arms. Tamar, Mary Ann, and I tried not to make a scene since we were older and were allowed to stay together. We went to our groups, but I felt nauseous and dizzy. I wondered if things would ever go back to the way they were—just us together as a family. Our group marched in single file down the stairs to breakfast. There was silence apart from the stomping of our feet.

"No one steps out of line," a man said. I was told he was our group shepherd. "And try to walk in sync." There were eight of us. I had a hard time synchronizing my steps with those of my peers. Tamar was close behind me. Clearly things were going to be much more regimented here than we were used to.

Our shepherd led us through the halls and down to the dining room, where breakfast waited on the tables: little white bowls of rice and plastic jugs of thick powdered milk. The eight of us were seated so tightly together I could feel Tamar's elbow nudge against my arm whenever she moved or took a bite. Auntie Joan was making the rounds.

"We don't have a lot of sugar, and milk powder is running low," she said when she stopped at our table. "So, eat sparingly.

And fill up on rice if you're still hungry. The Lord provided plenty of rice!"

(I later learned that food we received for free from the markets. We had fish and tofu in plentiful supply, but luxuries like sugar and oil—which we sometimes had to buy—were in short supply and had to be used sparingly or we'd run out.)

"If you eat the cereal fast enough," one of the kids said, "then you can taste the sugar before it dissolves."

The boy was skinny. The bones of his elbows jutted out, his face was sunken in and gaunt, his hair thin. I learned that he and his family of six had just come from India, where food and other resources were even scarcer than they were here.

As I stared into my bowl at the clumps of plain white rice that sat like mountains above the milk, I realized there would be no more family walks to fields with eucalyptus trees or hikes to the ditch or playing make-believe at the manger. I was in a new, unfamiliar world. I couldn't bring myself to take a bite. I was already exhausted. When our shepherd told us to go to our rooms for Word Time, I still hadn't touched my cereal. I looked down at my bowl, where the small pile of brown sugar had dissolved.

CHAPTER 13

I QUICKLY LEARNED THE NEW routine that would dictate my life. Reveille was at seven A.M., and by seven thirty sharp our room was immaculate and spotless, the bed sheets unwrinkled and spread tightly. We gathered ourselves into neat rows and stood at attention, each line containing eight to twelve children, determined by age. We stood shortest to tallest, so I was somewhere in the back with Tamar close behind me. We marched in single file. "Hup-two-three-four. God is not a fan of war." Like soldiers, we filed down the stairs and through the hall for mealtimes.

As we marched I often heard sounds coming from the narrow, screen-covered windows at the top of the walls. They were the sounds of adult excitement: women moaning, beds creaking, and men breathing heavily. The adults were participating in God's love, as they were encouraged to do unstintingly. We kids marched on, chanting. "I'm a soldier in the Lord's army, the sword of the Spirit is in my hand."

Breakfast was thick rice porridge or powdered eggs that had been scrambled into a curdled consistency to stretch the protein further, and steamed rice sopped with soy sauce. No complaints. No criticisms. No one was allowed to talk. Don't speak unless spoken to. Children must be seen, not heard. During lunch, we slapped the boiled tofu we hated to the bottom of the table, where it stuck like gum. When it splattered to the floor, we pretended we didn't know how it got there. We had plenty of tofu and rice in supply so we balled up the rice and had a food fight when the adults weren't looking, until someone got hauled off to the bathroom for a spanking and the rest of us laughed like hyenas.

We had three meals a day and a snack in the afternoon. The snack consisted of stale army crackers or sometimes cookies and milk. The milk was made from mixing milk powder with water, but we found a way to turn it into a sweet sugary treat by not adding any water. Instead the powder stuck to our gums and made clomping sounds as we worked it into a smooth consistency. Since we weren't used to sweets, we'd sneak out of our beds in the middle of the night and go to the kitchen to stuff our faces with spoonfuls of chalky, dehydrated milk from the great big barrels until we'd hear a noise and run back to bed, our bellies satisfied from the sweetness of the milk powder.

Everything we ate was donated to us: leftovers and extra inventory from the local markets. It was often stale or rotten, but we kids didn't mind since the fermented fruit was sweeter. Sometimes we were blessed with an overabundance of rotten bananas. The kids were called out to the garage to peel and bag as many as we could so they could be frozen for banana bread. The dark molasses we usually used as a sweetener was thick and sweet but had a bitter tinge. We had to boil it before eating it. We later learned that it was meant for racehorses, not humans. One time the molasses boiled over onto the kitchen counter and floor. We scooped up the molasses that had spilled onto the counter and put it back in the pot to be boiled again.

■ ■

A MAN NAMED UNCLE STEVEN Bald became our group shepherd at Khorat, which was starting to feel more like a permanent home than a temporary one. Most of the adults there came from countries besides America—France, Australia, Thailand, the Philippines—and had thick accents and exotic faces, but Uncle Steven spoke plain American English. He was shiny-bald, with just a strip of dirty-blond hair that wrapped around the base of his head. With so many members coming and going, and with Steven being a common name, he was given the nickname Uncle Steven Bald. Most of the adults were required to abandon their given names and choose new Bible names when they joined the Children of God. Adopted names and nicknames were common. We abandoned surnames entirely.

We'd been living in our new home a few weeks when Uncle Steven pulled Tamar, Mary Ann, and me aside. He said he had an important matter to discuss and that Mom would be there too. It was late afternoon. Most of the other kids were outside for their afternoon hour of play, and the sun was dropping low through the blinds.

I had my dolly with me. Tamar, Mary Ann, and I carried our dollies everywhere. They were our comfort in our unfamiliar new home. Uncle Steven sat down and said a prayer. He clasped his hands and met us at eye level.

"Girls," he said, "it's time for you to forsake your dollies."

"We have to give them away?" I was appalled. My dolly had been a gift from my Aunt Mary in California, who now lived in Japan with her husband and five children. She reminded me of the days in California when it was just my family, cousins, and relatives. My dolly had flown with us across the ocean. I'd played with her for hours in the backyard of our house in Udon Thani. I had held her close when we had fled the officials. She had parted lips, a tiny thumb, eyes with long lashes, and eyelids that opened and closed. She was nameless and bald—with crevices carved into her head instead of hair—but she remained my best companion. Tamar and I often compared our two dollies: they were identical, like us, but also unique in their own way— mine with a tiny dot on her left thumb, hers with a broken eyelid that wouldn't open. Mary Ann's dolly had wisps of blond hair, just like Mary Ann.

"That's what Jesus wants of you, yes," Uncle Steven Bald said. "You're old enough now. It's time you become more dedicated disciples for Jesus."

Mary Ann shuffled in her seat. I looked at Mom. She nodded. Her brown hair hung over her shoulders and her smile was as beautiful as ever.

I knew what "forsaking all" meant. It was a part of everyday speech for us. It was something the adults did when they joined the Children of God: renounced their physical possessions and families. They often told stories—"testimonies"—of how they had given up their families and dreams, their education, money, parents, boyfriends, girlfriends, fiancés, to be part of the Children of God mission. Nothing in the outside world—the "system"— could compare to the fulfillment of following their beloved prophet, Father David, and giving their lives in service to God and doing his work.

I clutched my dolly closer until I felt her little air-filled body deflate in my grasp. She was the only thing I owned.

"God never takes anything away without giving us something better," Mom said.

"Like how God gave you Becky after you had to deliver a dead baby in California?" Mary Ann was developing a habit of asking blunt questions.

Mom nodded.

Uncle Steven Bald had been holding a black leather-bound Bible on his lap. Now he flipped through the silver-edged pages and landed on a bookmarked verse.

"Hallelujah. Praise the Lord. Luke 14:33 says, 'So likewise whosoever he be of you that forsaketh not all that he hath, he cannot be my disciple.' Did you hear that girls? '*All* that he hath.'"

Uncle Steven handed us each a little booklet filled with passages of verses. I saw more verses from the gospel of Luke: "If any man come to me and hate not his father, and mother, and wife, and children, and brethren, and sisters, yea, and his own life also, he cannot be my disciple." Another one said, "And whosoever doth not bear his cross, and come after me, cannot be my disciple." My heart started thumping. I felt the back of my eyelids get hot. I had been taught that Jesus was all about love and forgiveness. I had never heard of these verses before. We promised Uncle Steven we would memorize these stern commandments. He said later there'd be a quiz.

I gave my dolly one last sip from her empty bottle and stroked her bald, rippled head. Hard as I tried to hold them back, tears welled in my eyes. I handed my dolly to Uncle Steven Bald. I looked at Tamar and Mary Ann. They were crying too. "Thank you, girls," he said. "And God *bless* you." He looked like he was on the verge of tears too. This happened often to the adults in the Family. Overtaken by euphoria, they were not sure if they were elated or sad. "Slain in the spirit," they called it, or "filled up on the Holy Ghost."

He deposited our three dollies in a large trash bag filled with other toys—kick balls, toy cars, Barbie dolls, and simple board games. Then he laid his hands over us and prayed one last time, asking God to rebuke any demons of selfishness, possessiveness, and greed that might have inhabited our minds, bodies, or spirits.

Even though I was supposed to keep my eyes closed during prayer time, they opened in a flash. Suddenly I was overcome by guilt. *Selfishness. Possessiveness. Greed.* I had not been aware of these demons before. I had not known I was selfish, possessive, or greedy. Where had these demons come from, and how could I get rid of them?

The next morning, during break time, I heard the wheels of the garbage truck squeaking to a slow halt in front of the gate. Tamar and I ran outside. I imagined chasing down the truck to find my dolly in a pile of rotting trash—her limbs all but demolished, her face battered and stained, her eyelids frozen shut, her eyelashes gone, her clothes torn—and rescuing her.

"I'm happy I didn't give her a name," I told Tamar as the garbage truck rolled away with our dollies inside. We held hands and waved to the truck that was long gone down the dirt road.

"Our dollies are garbage now."

"No, they're not," Tamar said. "They're in heaven now." Her smile made me want to believe her.

CHAPTER 14

I**T TURNED OUT WE WOULD** soon be moving from Khorat after all. The leaders—Father David's seconds-in-command, who mapped out where families should go—had decided it. Like human chess pieces, we relocated at the orders of these invisible masters. Father David was the mastermind. I was beginning to see that my family was just a small piece of a much larger, grander puzzle over which neither I nor my parents had control. Although Mom and Dad never talked about leaving the Family, I sometimes wondered if they ever thought about going back to California, like I did.

Upon leaving Khorat, we took a ferry across Pak Prah Strait in the Andaman Sea to Phuket Island. A retired high-ranking army colonel from southern Thailand had been persuaded by some of the Thai aunties to let a few of us stay at his island property for reduced rent. Father David said that because we were on a mission to save the world, people would offer us gifts, and we should accept them readily. They were blessings from God and a sign that He was pleased with our work. The colonel certainly never knew how many people would be staying at his luxury estate.

The city we traveled to was worlds away from the northern Thai countryside I had known. It boasted luxury resorts; white-sand beaches strewn with bungalows, and upmarket penthouse suites. American expats and aging tourists had on their arms pretty young Thai girls who I later learned were prostitutes. Fishermen timed their excursions with the tides to gather the day's catch. Neon "Open All Night" signs blinked in the windows of restaurants and bars. Beaches were crowded with scantily clad vacationers reclining on bright towels and poolside chairs.

When we arrived at the colonel's estate, we were greeted by the fresh sea air and a cool breeze. Wisps of white cirrus clouds drifted in the sky. I felt like I had been transported to an enchanted land. The house was a one-story estate set amidst hills of poppies and baby palm trees. The entrance featured two heavy wood-frame doors, marble pillars, and a sprawling wraparound terrace. In the front yard an orchid garden sprang from a log, showing off dancing queen flowers in full bloom.

Tamar and I ran through the spacious yard with its rolling hills. Orange poppies with buttery-smooth petals and powdery pollen grew on a mound. Vibrant butterflies with chalky blue and yellow wings that opened and closed with clocklike precision stalked the tips of bougainvillea blossoms. Tamar showed me how to catch a butterfly by holding still until it landed on my outstretched hand. Its wings were smooth and velvety, just like the flowers. Mary Ann was busy feeding four fuzzy chicks that resided behind a wire fence. Their fluff had been dyed bright yellow, pink, green, and blue. Tamar rubbed a soft orchid petal between her fingertips.

"Dad said we have to wait for the other families to arrive before we get settled in."

It was the nicest house I had ever seen, and I couldn't believe we would be living there. There was a master bedroom and five additional bedrooms. The walls in the common area were made entirely of glass. The kitchen had a wide center counter, spacious cupboards, and big windows. Stairs led to an open dining room with heavy oak tables. On the wall in the master bedroom hung the traditional portrait of the king and the queen. Every residence and business in Thailand was required to have one. We had learned the king's name and could recite it on command: "Phra Bat Somdet Phra Poramintharamaha Bhumibol Adulyadej." It was one of the few things I knew how to say in Thai. In the homes we visited on witnessing trips, I had examined the king's face in his portraits—his wide-set jaw, prominent ears, and soft lips. The queen had light skin and pink lipstick. An offering of fruit and flower baskets lay close to the portraits, and incense smoke curled around their somber faces.

Higher still on the wall in the colonel's home, higher than the king and queen, hung a painting of the colonel himself—a daring show of indiscretion and arrogance. In Thai culture, it was a sign of disrespect to position your head above someone else's— even customary to bow your head as a youngster when walking in front of elders. We kids whispered murmurs of concern and shame for this officer who thought he was more lofty than the esteemed monarchs.

We would be living with three other families, Dad told us: Uncle Shem and Auntie Joy and their nine children, Uncle Paul and Auntie Rachel and their four boys, Uncle French John and Auntie Meekness and their five children. A few other single, young adults, whom we called YAs, would also reside there. On the night they arrived, the adults gathered for a meeting to pray and discuss the living arrangements. Tamar, Mary Ann, and I made friends with Christina and Jeremy, Shem and Joy's oldest kids. Since living quarters were tight, as always, we shared a room.

The next morning a chart was tacked up on the kitchen wall detailing a weekly routine and listing everyone's name and their family symbol. Our family was represented by a star. The adults were assigned daily tasks: Uncle Paul was our group shepherd, Auntie "Swiss" Joy took care of the younger kids, Uncle "Thai" Abe was the home cook. Auntie Peace, Uncle Shem, and Auntie Rachel rotated between witnessing trips and stints spent collecting donations and networking for support and supplies. Mom and 2Dad were assigned as home shepherds.

Some adults were categorized as "scary" by the kids. They were strict disciplinarians—like Uncle Stephan, who was French and wore a thick ring on his middle finger. He was known to give knuckle sandwiches during lunch—a swift, unexpected knuckle delivered to the middle of the head when someone talked out of turn or laughed. The clunky ring felt like it would leave a dent in your head for the rest of the afternoon. If that wasn't enough to make us lose our "attitude," he'd take us to the bathroom for a swift paddle to the bottom. Mealtimes were often interrupted by the sounds of a child being paddled in the bathroom. The remaining kids at the table either laughed uncontrollably or sat frozen in silence.

We kids knew to stay clear of the "strict" adults and to avoid talking back or questioning anything they said or did. Mom and Dad weren't considered strict, but they weren't always around like they had been in Udon Thani. Some adults, like Auntie Meekness, Uncle Paul, and Auntie "Na" Peace, were nice. I gravitated toward them as replacements for Mom and Dad when they were absent.

I had hoped that as home shepherds, Mom and Dad would spend most of their time at our home, but they often had to be away for weeks at a time to attend trainings. The trainings took place at larger homes that were located in the central region, near Bangkok, and that had more frequent contact with the leaders at headquarters. The trainings were to help my parents focus on their service to Jesus and their devotion to prayer without the distraction of taking care of the house and their kids, who from what I could tell continued to take a backseat in their priorities.

CHAPTER 15

AS MEMBERS OF THE FAMILY, we were expected to "share" our relatives with each other. Auntie Meekness was one of my favorites. She wasn't our group shepherd, but sometimes she joined us outside for afternoon recess. She had been a ballerina, but she didn't talk much about her past, which she, like all adult members, had "forsaken" when she joined the Children of God. She had a strong French accent and crescent-shaped eyes above high, round cheekbones. She wore bangs that made her look youthful, and her white panties showed beneath her skirt when she demonstrated how to do cartwheels.

I knew what a ballerina was because we kids were allowed to watch the Russian ballet *Swan Lake* since it was a powerful

story of good versus evil. The women danced around the stage
with their muscular legs and white stockings and feathery hair-
pieces. I wanted to be one of those dancers because when they
were suspended in the air they were free, and when they stood
on point I thought their feet could never grow old—like the
bound feet of the Chinese girls in *The Inn of Sixth Happiness*. Of
all the things the adults forsook to become God's children—
families and fiancés and fancy cars—I thought Auntie Meekness
had given up the most because she could have been like one
of the girls in *Swan Lake,* a human butterfly, light as a feather,
graceful as water.

One afternoon during recess Auntie Meekness taught
Tamar and me the plié and how to point our toes and do a
spinning jump, landing with our heels and toes in perfect
alignment. I practiced fifth position on the squishy grass. I
lined up my left heel in front of my right big toe. With my
hips turned out and my freckled knees pointed in opposite
directions, my legs felt awkward. I raised my arms to a tree-
hugging position. Shoulders down. Head high. Neck long. My
arms felt heavy. First, she showed us how to jump up and land
gracefully. I bent my knees to catch some momentum and then
pushed off. Toes pointed. Collarbone even. Not looking down.
Petit saut. Next, we learned how to scissor our legs in midair.
Changement de pieds—"change of feet." I had found my niche. I
wanted to be a ballerina.

Get-Out was an hour-long daily recess when we were
allowed to be outside. We rotated in shifts to avoid revealing to
the neighbors how many people were crammed together in one
house. During Get-Out, Tamar and I worked hard at ballet. We
perfected our pliés and balanced on one leg, pointing our toes
and learning to scissor our legs in the air. Tamar's feet were big
and bony. Mine were smaller and more delicate, but still big. We

were awkward and clumsy but diligent and serious in our practice. The earth squished under our toes whenever we landed from a *changement de pieds*. The grass stained our heels.

■ ■

ONE DAY MOM HAD A brilliant idea. "Let's fill the master bedroom with water and make our own indoor swimming pool!" she said triumphantly. Sometimes she'd try to implement fun activities for us kids—arts and crafts in the evening or predawn picnics on the beach. Her ideas would get shot down by another home shepherd, and she had to fight to make them work or abandon them altogether.

She explained that the master bedroom, where the colonel's arrogant portrait hung, was originally meant to be a swimming pool, but midway through construction the architects changed their minds and decided to turn it into the master bedroom instead. It was sunken lower than the other rooms. To enter it you had to walk down a set of four concrete steps. The room was a giant perfect square with one door that led outside and another sliding glass door that led to the living room. The wall to the living room was made entirely of glass and was covered with a thin curtain. Around the perimeter was a carpeted ledge where we often sat for Word Time and School Time. The rest of the room was laid with smooth white tiles. This gave Mom the brilliant idea that it could double as a swimming pool, like the architects had originally intended.

We ran a long hose from an outdoor faucet. "This'll be just like swimming in the ocean!" she said promisingly. She was wearing her work clothes—shorts with a sleeveless shirt and a scarf tied around her head. I believed her. I especially liked when Mom was involved in planning our daily activities. When she did get her way, we often found ourselves leaving the house before the sun came up and having six A.M. picnics on the beach or staying in the ocean far longer than the time we were allotted in our daily schedule. I knew Mom had a hand in negotiating these adventures.

We poured water into the room until it was knee deep. We dressed in our swimming clothes. We took turns in groups wading around, our white swim clothes ballooning above the water like parachutes. We raced from end to end and propelled ourselves from the sides with our feet. The force sent us zooming across the pool; we pretended we were professional swimmers. The tiles were smooth and the water was warm. Uncle Paul and Mom sat in the shallow water while we splashed around like babies in a bathtub.

At the end of the day, when it was time to drain the water, we came across a problem. In her haste to make our day fun, Mom didn't think about how we would empty the pool and forgot to check for a drain. We looked in the corners for a silver grid. There was none. We searched the middle of the room to see if the floor slanted downward to a vacuum that could suck the water underground. No luck.

Mom announced that we'd have to empty the pool the old fashioned way, bucket by bucket. I was thrilled that the fun would continue into late evening. I could tell the other kids were too. We found buckets and spent the better part of the evening ladling water from the room and pouring it onto the grass in the yard. It was the most fun I'd had in a long time—since being back in Udon Thani.

Everyone seemed to like Mom. She was one of the favorite aunties in every home we lived in, even though she could sometimes be strict. *If Mom could be just* my *mom,* I thought as the sun disappeared into the night, *and if we didn't have to share brothers and sisters and parents and aunts and uncles, then maybe we could be a family again.* Maybe then my life would be perfect.

CHAPTER 16

IN A WAY, MOM AND Uncle Steven Bald were right. When I gave away my dolly, I got something else in return. I had developed quite a creative streak. Back in Udon Thani, Dad had taught us to sketch real-life images. We sat for hours trying to draw the perfect hand, and Dad's always turned out the best. I thought he had the gentlest hands. "Artist hands," he called them. Mine were similar—delicate but ancient looking with deep wrinkles and long, slender fingers.

Although Dad didn't talk much about his family outside the Children of God, he'd sometimes sneak in stories about his dad, our grandpa, who had been a makeup artist and worked on Hollywood sets for elaborate movie productions. He even had his own production company, with seven artists who worked under him. "He had an eye for design but wasn't the best businessman," Dad would say.

Dad's mom, my grandma Mary Ann, wrote Hallmark cards after she divorced my grandpa when Dad was nine. "She had a way with words," Dad said sometimes, staring off into the distance at nothing. I imagined her during her last days when she was sick with emphysema, sitting alone in her room chain-smoking cigarettes, a yellow cloud of smoke forming a ring around the bright floral stationary, writing cheerful birthday greetings and thoughtful get-well notes. She died the year I was born.

Most of Dad's brothers, my uncles, were also talented musicians and lyricists. Uncle Bird wrote songs for the Children of God; Uncle Dave recorded his own albums. My Uncle Bob, whom I'd met once in California, was a published poet and lived in Oregon. He was one of the few of my dad's siblings who had never joined the Children of God and had what Dad called "a bit of a drinking problem."

Artistry ran in our family, I knew. I loved sketching faces, the second hardest thing to draw besides hands and feet. In Phuket I could practice the drawing skills I'd learned. I began sketching the ornaments embellishing the colonel's estate. Impressionist paintings of the Thai countryside hung in the dining room. Stained-glass vases sat empty on wooden coffee tables. A dazzling chandelier dangled overhead in the living room. White tablecloths embroidered with orchids and native birds decorated the wooden tables. I began sketching nature—charcoals of birds and butterflies complete with details of the veins in the monarch's wings. I shaded the dull fluff that feathered the ears of sparrows and looked like holes hidden behind grey lint. I kept my sketches in a secret hiding place under my bed.

I began to notice other kinds of art too. Usually we were only allowed to read Father David's word or the Bible, but there was a book in the house called the *Rhyme Book*. It was a collection of poems written by nonmembers (called "systemites" within the

Family), but Father David had approved them for us to read. He had a deep reverence for poetry and sometimes spoke in rhyme and sonnets when he was receiving prophecies from God, glorifying the woman's body, or damning America and the West. The production team in Japan had compiled and edited the *Rhyme Book*. It had a cream-colored cover and was full of poetry accompanied by pictures. My favorite poem was Joyce Kilmer's "Trees." I took to the order of rhyming words. I wanted to create things. Even though we had so little to create with, I had made a little notebook by stapling a cardboard cover around some lined pages. The edges were crooked and the binding was bulky where the staples held the pages together.

One day when Get-Out was over, all the kids were rounded up to go inside for shower and dinnertime. Dusk was my favorite time of the day, with its haunting sky that seemed to close in on me as darkness approached. The temperature lowered with the setting of the sun, and my skin felt cool. Right before the bell rang, a few of us who wanted to stay longer ran to the farthest corner of the yard and hid behind hibiscus bushes or ripe mango trees. The yard was large so we would be the last ones inside, trudging in reluctantly, taking as long as we could, like children who have been told to get out of a swimming pool on a hot summer day. I paced in circles around the hill of bright orange poppies in bloom. No one was in sight.

That was the day I first wrote something of my own. It was a poem. I was seven. I still remember it word for word:

One day I was walking through the garden,
Very, very pardoned.
I wondered why this and that;
I guess I'll know when He comes back.
I wondered why the flowers blossomed,
Only in spring,

And never forgotten.
I wondered why it rains in May,
And butterflies seem so gay.
Then one day Jesus came,
And he did explain.
He curled every pearl.
He crossed every *t,*
And he explained it all.

I tucked my poem away. The sky was getting darker, and I knew I shouldn't be caught outside alone. As I turned to go inside, I thought I heard a noise coming from the kitchen window to my left. When I looked closer I saw nothing but the swaying of the light blue curtains.

Before going to bed I stashed my poem in my secret hiding place alongside my sketches. I knew I could be punished for being creative. When I woke up the next morning I reached under the bed to make sure my things were still safe where I had left them. Tamar was sleeping on a mattress next to my bed, snoring slightly with her mouth parted and her legs splayed. I brushed my hand along the floor tiles, which were cold even though the morning air was hot and dry. I swept beneath the bed as far as I could, but I felt nothing except granules of dirt on the cold tile. I hauled myself over the edge of my mattress to see if they'd been moved in the night or if I'd accidentally pushed them into another corner.

"Do you know where our things went?" I asked Tamar, who was stirring now as she woke up.

"Where what went?" She opened her eyes.

"Our things," I said. "I put my poem underneath the bed with my sketches."

"I'll check," she said.

She slid under the bed to have a better look.

There was nothing, she said. They were gone.

CHAPTER 17

FATHER DAVID BEGAN TO ENCOURAGE proper schooling for us kids. We turned the master bedroom into a schoolroom. If we ever had a raid, we'd be able to state with confidence, "Yes, we have a proper education." I was learning to say we were "missionaries" and that I was "homeschooled."

With no money to buy desks and chairs, we sat on the floor during school time with our legs crossed and backs slouched over like we did during Word Time, when the adults were going on about God and Father David's latest prophecy. In the master bedroom two posters decorated the white walls, along with the colonel's portrait and the portraits of the monarchs. One was a map of the world with pastel colors separating one continent from the next. Dotted lines set borders for countries and states, and solid lines divided the land from the water. The other was a diagram of the Thai alphabet, complete with pictographs and phonetic structures. I learned the entire Thai alphabet, beginning with *ko kai,* illustrated by a colorful rooster, with a shiny red and green mane of feathers, for "chicken" or *kai.* Next came *kho khai, khoh khuat,* and the forty-four consonants with their fancy loops and twirling arrangements.

The Thai vowels were difficult to master. Some of them hung in the air above the consonants or dangled low below their tails or sandwiched combinations of letters to form soundable words. Tones had the freedom to transform a word at will, and we often sat around during lunch and mused over the word *ma,* which could mean five different things—from "come" to "horse" to "dog"—depending on whether the speaker's tone was rising, falling, high, or stable.

Auntie Peace was Thai and she taught us the Thai alphabet as part of our daily school schedule. In proper salutation and as a form of respect, we called her "Na Peace," *Na* meaning "Auntie" in Thai. The word *Na* had a rising tone, but *Peace* stayed flat and monotone, like most other English words. Na Peace had long black hair, full lips, and a rather squat face.

Our schoolbooks were the Super Workbook series, which contained an entire grade's worth of material in a single thick book with colorful covers, which made them look like giant blocks of candy. The fourth-grade workbook was orange with a shiny cover and chunky lettering on the front. It was mine to own and it was my favorite. We used pencil to fill in the answers, so when one group of kids finished with the workbook they could erase the answers and pass them down to the next group of kids. Because school was given relatively low priority, and we spent most of our days in Word Time or prayer or cleaning house and doing chores, I never got past the first few pages of the fifth-grade workbook, which was blue.

Movie Day happened once a week. In the afternoon we'd watch a film from the Recommended List. If there was cane sugar in the sugar barrel on Movie Day, we ate sugar-glazed, air-popped popcorn. The movies on the Recommended List tended toward plotlines in which kids were taken away from their parents. We all knew very well this was to prepare us for a raid or the Great Apocalypse, when we'd have to disperse and our parents wouldn't be there to protect us. We would be called on to fulfill our destiny and be strong, like Heaven's Boy and Heaven's Girl, the heroes of a series of "futuristic, prophetic" stories for children written by Father David.

There were about ten movies approved for us kids, including *101 Dalmatians, Annie,* and the *The Inn of Sixth Happiness.* We'd watch them over and over, until we knew how to stay calm if we were ever separated from our parents. These musicals, Disney cartoons, and true-life stories showed us that families being torn apart was a normal occurrence even in the system—so we had nothing to fear. For history, we watched *Marco Polo, The Ten Commandments,* and *Jesus of Nazareth. Pinocchio* was also on the Recommended List, but when we reached the part where he enters into the land of frivolity and vanity, the adult watching with us would press the fast forward button and put a pillow over the TV screen so we wouldn't get any ideas about the tempting world outside that leads Pinocchio into the belly of the whale, like Jonah. As I grew older, the repertoire of acceptable movies expanded to include *Six Weeks, To Sir with Love,* and *Les Misérables.*

Aside from what I saw in the rural countryside or the bustling city streets while out witnessing, or on visa trips, or en route to a new home, those movies were all I knew of the outside world.

CHAPTER 18

WE WEREN'T ALLOWED TO LEAVE the house during the day. Too dangerous! Someone might see us. Someone might catch us. Someone might take us away.

I began to think more about the world outside those walls—how big it must've been, how many people were in it, people I would never meet and who never knew I existed.

At night, I would stare up at the moon, mesmerized by the bright, silver ball with its crevices and caverns resting on a of black. Father David said that the Heavenly City lived on the moon, and that's where we were all headed once the Rapture came, after the Great Apocalypse. That's where the Marriage Supper of the

Lamb would take place: in a big yellow pyramid that would land inside the moon after the Great Tribulation.

Father David was obsessed with heaven. In his top-secret home his artists sketched pictures of heaven to be included in his MO Letters, comic books, and colorful posters so we'd have a clear picture of our future. Father David's lunar heaven was full of women wearing minimal clothing. Their see-through white garments draped delicately over their bodies. Their legs peeked out from slits that went clear up to their hipbones.

In my mind I played the scenario of arriving in heaven thousands of times over the course of many nights before bed while listening to Father David's tape recordings. Imagining heaven made the death part feel manageable. First, upon my arrival I would be given angelic wings. Then I'd be granted unearthly superpowers: I could fly at the speed of light, make myself invisible at will, zap my enemies with thunderbolts, and call down lightning from the sky. I'd be able to walk through walls and hide from my enemies. When I wasn't busy wielding my superpowers, I could play in lush tropical gardens with rushing waterfalls and orchards of fruit trees. *And* I'd get to stay "forever young." Whatever age I was when I arrived in heaven, that's the age I would stay forever, Father David said. I would never have to grow old!

But the part I was most excited about was that when I got there I would be reunited with my family. Then we could stay together. We would never have to be apart again. At night, as I lay in my bed, I convinced myself that heaven would make the Great Tribulation worth it.

"How the heck do you think we're all gonna fit up there?" I asked Tamar one night. She was in her bunk bed leafing through an old volume of MO Letters. She put the book down and came over to look out the window with me. She leaned over to peer outside. All the other kids were getting ready for bed, but since we got ready fast we had a moment to ourselves.

"Where did you learn a word like *heck?*" she asked once we were so close we could hear each other whisper. "What's it mean?"

"It's an almost bad word," I whispered, trying to keep my voice low.

I knew that Father David said *fuck* and *shit* a lot in his letters to damn America and to talk about sex, but they were banned from our vocabulary or we'd get punished. We kids learned replacement words like *heck* and *shucks* and *darn* and used them freely whenever we were out of earshot from the adults.

"You better not say it too loud," Tamar whispered. "Or else you might get your mouth washed out with soap."

"Shucks," I said, and we giggled.

She looked back at the moon. "I don't know how the heck we're gonna fit up there," she said, answering my question and emphasizing the forbidden word. Her eyes widened.

I thought hard for a minute. "There's a lot of people on Earth," I said. "At least a million."

"Maybe more," Tamar said. "That's a lot of zeroes."

She showed me an encyclopedia. Under *A* for *astronomy* there was a picture of the moon and the earth, along with a diagram comparing the shape and size of the two.

"The moon's much smaller than the Earth," she said, pointing to the graph. The grid in the encyclopedia had a photo of the moon. It looked like a cratered crumb that had fallen off Earth's swirly mass. Suddenly I felt small.

"I wonder who's going to heaven and who'll be left behind to burn in hell or suffer forever in the fire pit of purgatory," I gasped.

"Father David says whoever isn't saved at the Great Apocalypse will get one last chance to repent, then all the sinners will either go to hell or suffer forever in purgatory. That's why we have to save *everybody*," Tamar said.

"Father David says there are lots of wars out there," I said. I was speaking louder now. "It's a scary, scary place. There are evil leaders like Hitler and Stalin who do bad, bad things."

She nodded. "Shh," she said, putting her finger to her lips. "You have to speak quietly, else someone might hear us."

"Father David said there are wars in the Middle East," I said, whispering now.

"Where's the Middle East?"

"I dunno. Somewhere near the Garden of Eden, I think. Father David said we'll be safe as long as we stay within the walls. Then we have nothing to worry about."

"We're safe?"

"Yeah."

"I don't like war."

"Me neither."

I remembered the letters I'd read in which Father David recounted the wars in the Middle East and elsewhere. He assured us there was no reason to leave the safety of our compounds. The world outside was doomed. He'd conduct desperate prayer meetings recorded by his faithful scribe, Maria, in his top-secret hideout. He'd speak in tongues and nearly go delirious pleading for God to strike Khomeini dead. He'd ramble on about leaders in Russia and the United States, praying that God would do them the justice they deserved.

Around this time, I began to form thoughts on my own, and it was on the rare moments when I was alone that these thoughts began to crystalize. As I looked up at the moon that night, I began to question the world outside of myself—I had questions about humanity, life, astronomy, and how things work. My thoughts were free to wander where they pleased, and Tamar was there to hear my musings and I hers.

"You know what else I wonder," Tamar said. "Sometimes I think about humans and if they will ever run out of air to breathe."

"Yeah," I agreed. "Or where does all the garbage go after the garbage collectors come in their honking trucks." She laughed that I said *honking*. I thought of my dolly, and I started to miss her.

I also thought a lot about why I was me and whether I'd chosen to be born and whether I could be someone else or if I would be stuck in this body forever.

Tamar told me she had a confession to make. "Promise you won't tell anyone?"

"Promise."

"I tried to make myself go to heaven once," she said.

"Why?"

"'Cause I thought it'd be fun. Heaven *is* fun. Plus," she said, "I didn't want to have to go through the Apocalypse." She paused for a moment and looked down at the hem of her nightgown. "It's scary."

"You mean the Antichrist?"

"Yeah."

"The Antichrist *is* scary," I said, "but heaven is going to be beautiful! That's what Father David says." We studied a colorful poster depicting heaven that was taped to the wall beside our bed. Children played in lush gardens and swam in crystal-clear lakes and rivers. We talked about the big golden pyramid and the complex design structure that had been revealed to Father David, with vast open-air living quarters and poolside lounge areas, where beautiful heavenly beings roamed freely in their see-through one-piece garments and muscular angels glided overhead. I thought about his letters and my dreams. "In order to go to heaven, you first have to die, though," I said. Now I was looking down instead of at Tamar.

"I know," she said. "It's not that easy."

"Why not?" I looked up at her.

"'Cause then you think about everyone you have to leave behind."

She was staring intently out the window into the night sky. Her hands were folded in her lap. She seemed to be keenly concentrating on something. When I turned my head to see what she was looking at, the moon had become a sliver behind a spray of branches, casting a silver glow onto the houses below.

CHAPTER 19

Good morning, God's children,
Take a look outside,
It's a new morning, it's a new li-ife.
Such a beautiful day outside.
Why not get up,
And go walking in the sunlight.
Reveille, reveille, time to rise, rise and shine.
Reveille, reveille, time to get Jesus on your mind.

SUN CAME STREAMING THROUGH THE kitchen windows. The
smell of steamed white rice and brown cane sugar coiled up the
stairway while an uncle sang reveille, reminding me that the day

belonged to God. I wondered if there would ever come a day that belonged to me.

I began to notice that our family was larger than most of the others in the home. Mikey was the latest addition to our rapidly growing clan. He was number eight. We called him "Little Man." He was the longest baby to date, with jet-black hair and fingers to match his body's length, like he was born to be a professional pianist.

In other large families, the children were more spaced out, with older children away doing missionary work in another country or grown and married with children. But in our family, John, the oldest, was barely twelve. You could tell that all of us kids came from Dad: we shared with him the Irish freckled skin, ski-slope noses, and distinct cowlick hairlines. Plus, there was no denying the Edwards demeanor: quiet, shy but intelligent, observant, sarcastic, and artistic—"armchair philosophers," my cousin Anthony called us.

Our parents made it clear they did not have or plan to have kids with other members. This news satisfied my sisters and me deeply. Most large families I knew were "mixed." A family of seven might have kids from three or four different continents, "with all the colors of the rainbow." Even though in his letters Father David encouraged adults to "share," and told us we were "one big happy family," our parents seemed to stick together, unlike most. And I could tell they still loved and were committed to each other.

Soon Mom was pregnant with number nine. That's when Dad called a family meeting to tell us that he and Mom were "going for the gold." "That means your mother and I are not planning to hold back anymore, and if God wants us to have lots of babies, then that's His will. We are only vessels of God's love. Are you guys ready for more brothers and sisters?"

"Going for the gold" meant adults were encouraged to use no birth control method of any kind. Members did have the option of going "bronze" or "silver" by using certain allowable birth control methods: condoms or pulling out or applying the rhythm method. (We'd read about these in the Story of Davidito series.) Still, settling for anything less than God's best was never worthy of praise or rewards in heaven.

I stared down at the glossy floorboards and in the cracks between them at the smooth grey rocks below. I wondered just how many children Mom was capable of bearing and if there would come a point when her body would just say no. I noticed she was often emotional and spent days in tears. When we'd ask her what was wrong she'd say it was because she was pregnant and pregnant women get emotional and cry a lot because of the hormones, but she never talked about solving the problem by not having more kids.

"Okay," we said.

I didn't mind being the big sister, but it didn't seem fair to bring more children into the world during a time like this. Their decision was more evidence to me that Mom and Dad's loyalty was to Father David rather than to us kids. I figured having more children meant we would have a grander army come the Great Apocalypse, when we'd have to hide out from the Antichrist deep in the mountains during the Great Tribulation. Outside, the sun smiled radiantly while a gentle breeze teased the surface of the turquoise-blue ocean.

After Mom had Suzy (number nine), she immediately became pregnant with Brian on a visa trip when she and Dad met up for one night after having been apart for months. We often joked about how fertile she was. "It's just God's way of blessing me," she'd say. "Just think, some people are unable to ever have kids."

Especially considering how fervently Father David encouraged procreation, I was beginning to see that he didn't encourage traditional family bonds. In his letters and teachings on family and on child care, it was clear that he thought any other kind of family competed with *the* Family. That was part of why adults were encouraged to share their love instead of sticking with a single partner. It was why everyone who joined the Family had to cut ties with those they'd left behind. Father David said the family unit was an impediment to God's work. We shouldn't put our selfish needs above God's calling. Commitment to family and domestic responsibilities took attention away from God's ultimate plan and was shunned. God was our first love and we were His sexy young bride, he'd often say, waiting to be wed to Him at the Marriage Supper of the Lamb, when we'd all be united forever in godly matrimony and holy bliss. There was no need to honor family ties or adhere to strict ancestral lineages.

Earlier that year Father David had ordered us to burn any photos depicting an outside relative. Mom kept one photograph of her parents, justifying it since their faces were not clearly visible. The photograph was yellow-stained and torn near the edges. In the photo, the grandfather I'd never met is lying on a reclining poolside lawn chair, lifting his left arm to cover his face. His skin is deeply bronzed in the midday sun. He's leaning toward my Mormor (the swedish name for my grandmother). They're both sunbathing near what looks to be a backyard pool. It's probably sometime in the late afternoon during high summer in Scandinavia—the Land of the Midnight Sun. Mormor is young and darkly tan and is wearing a blue one-piece bathing suit. Her skin is olive and her hair is brown and thick, like Mom's, and she's covering part of her face and laughing, probably at something my grandfather just said. That was the only image I had of Mom's parents.

I didn't know much more about my grandfather. I knew from the photograph that he liked to sunbathe until his skin turned the color of copper. I knew that, like my Uncle Bob on my dad's side, he had a bit of a drinking problem. He used to wake Mom and her younger sister, Eva, in the middle of the night in his drunken rages, yelling for no reason at all. I knew that Denmark was a ferry ride away from the southernmost tip of Sweden, and whenever Mom wanted to get away she paid the ferry conductor a shiny coin.

Most kids born into the Children of God never knew of or met their grandparents. My Grandma Mary Ann, Dad's mom, died the year I was born, so I never met her. And I had been too young to remember Mom's mom, Mormor, who took Tamar and me to a real church ceremony in Sweden to get baptized when we were newborns. We wore long, white, flowing dresses. After our family left Sweden for Mexico City, Mom hardly spoke to her family. One morning she told me she had received a letter from her mother informing her that her father had died. "He died from cancer," she said. She shook her head and looked down. Tears welled up in her eyes. I could tell she missed him.

I knew there was no time for me to cry in the Family, especially over someone I'd never known. After a hearty breakfast of rice cereal with powdered milk and cane sugar, we marched in line to our designated groups. The adults were assigned to their duties, and some children were hustled away for special disciplinary action. I shivered whenever I heard my peers being beaten.

During recess I paced along the balcony overlooking the sprawling yard. To my right a white drained bathtub where babies sometimes played sat under the shade of a ripe mango tree. The sun beat down, ricocheting off the fat blades of grass that snaked through the lawn. Plump, fluorescent green flies with purple iridescent wings buzzed outside the screen doors. A young boy Timmy was being beaten again, and with each lash of the belt he let out a cry that sounded like a war whoop. I felt my insides tighten up. There was nothing I could do but be as quiet and still as possible so I wouldn't have to endure the same punishment.

Beads of sweat formed on my forehead and pasted my bangs to the side of my head. My heart was racing. I peered into the distance and saw Mom's figure. She had been given the day off to grieve and was sitting outside on a lawn chair, alone. It was high noon. Mom sat with her legs crossed. Her olive skin reflected the sharp rays of the sun. She sat isolated, in quarantine, no one to talk to and no one to share her grief. There was a part of me that wanted to grieve when I realized Mom was also someone's daughter.

Tamar appeared behind me.

"What's Mom doing out there all by herself?" she said.

"She's crying."

"Why?" Tamar said.

"'Cause her daddy just died," I said. "She told me this morning."

"I'd cry if *my* daddy died," she said.

"He's *my* daddy too. Not just yours. I'd cry too if he died," I said. We kids often playfully argued over ownership of *our* parents ("How dare you say 'my' dad?"). I paused for a moment to think. "At least we all get to go to heaven together when the End Time comes. That way we don't have to lose Mommy or Daddy first."

"Yeah," Tamar said. Her face was pressed against the thin screen that covered the window, and she ran her fingers along its jagged edges.

"Do you think she's gonna fly back to Sweden for his funeral?" I asked. I imagined what a funeral in Sweden might look like: a gathering of bereaved people huddled together on a soft blanket of snow dressed in their best church clothes—black tuxedos, ruffled taffeta dresses, and low hats to conceal their mourning faces. They grieved over the one thing they had in common: a cold body slowly being lowered into the ground with an extensive system of rope-and-chain pulleys. The minister would say, "From dust thou art to dust thou shalt return," and mourners would pour handfuls of dirt over the shiny brass coffin.

"Probably not," Tamar said. "I don't think we have the money for a plane ticket to Sweden."

"Plus, Mom hadn't spoken to her dad in years," I said.

"I just thought of something," Tamar said. She took a deep breath. "What if Father David dies. What will happen then? He must be as old as our grandpa."

"Father David's not gonna die," I said. "We're all going to heaven first." I looked over the balcony to the distance at Mom again. She was rocking her body back and forth, stopping to wipe tears from her face as she cried. On a table next to her lay some Family literature—Daily Mights, Daily Breads, and MO Letters. Those kinds of things comforted her.

"Do you think Mommy missed her daddy before he died?" Tamar said.

"I don't know," I said. I shrugged. "Maybe when you become an adult you stop missing your parents altogether." I wondered if that was why they joined the Children of God in the first place—to find a new family.

"I'll never stop missing Mommy and Daddy," I said. "Even if I get older."

"Me neither," Tamar said. "Even if we become adults."

CHAPTER 20

IN THE EARLY DAYS OF his movement, Father David celebrated the sinner. But now, self-improvement had become a
defining component of his culture, and we kids were reminded
every day of our faults and inadequacies on a handmade poster
called the demerit chart. We became accustomed to scheduled
punishments or humiliations, often without knowing what we
had done wrong. We also became used to unexpected and erratic
outbursts of discipline.

One night before bedtime, Uncle Peter was reading stories
from the Heaven's Girl series. They were illustrated and compiled
in what could be described as an apocalyptic sex comic book.
Heaven's Girl parted the Red Sea like Moses and flirted with young

soldiers. The character's real name was Marie Claire. She looked just like Mama Maria, with long black hair, a pretty face tapering to a delicate chin, and slender limbs. In one story Heaven's Girl gets cornered by an army of men. In order to escape, she opens her legs wide and lets some of the men lie on top of her while the rest of the men watch.

Father David said that we should strive to be more like Heaven's Girl. In the comic books she wore a small, white, flimsy dress that clung tightly to her teenage body. A braided belt held the costume together. Her nipples were always visible through her dress. Her hair was tied back in a long tress that whipped across her bottom whenever she fought. She was a warrior. She wore sandals with straps that crisscrossed up to her knees, accentuating her legs. Heaven's Girl could perform miraculous feats and had superpowers: besides parting the water, she could control minds and make herself invisible. I fantasized about having a pair of those sandals for my own, even if I had to become Heaven's Girl to get them.

Uncle Peter had to sit on one of the beds with no top bunk because he was tall. I sat on a top bunk with my back pressed against the wall. I was wearing my one-piece nightie with elastic red ruffles around the hem, collar, and sleeves. I loved that nightie. It almost resembled a dress, and it was the only almost-dress I owned. The ruffles tickled my arms and legs, and it had pictures of dancing hearts and happy stick figures that kept me entertained during Word Time.

Uncle Peter read stories to us about the Great Tribulation and the "seven signs of the times" that we should always be on the lookout for—among them, earthquakes, violence, drought, floods, wars, and pestilence. Baby geckos scurried along the shiny white walls, stopping to zap out their tongues and gobble up whatever insects got in their way.

"There shall be wars and rumors of war," Uncle Peter read in a calm voice. I had the whole chapter of Matthew 24 memorized and could recite it on command.

As Uncle Peter read, I felt a tug at my back. I looked down. Karen, a girl my age, was on the bottom bunk and pulling on my nightie. I tried to ignore her. She tugged again. I brushed at her hand to make her stop, and when I looked up I saw Uncle Peter coming my way. He was a big man with bulging arms and a muscular chest. He was wearing a sleeveless shirt and he towered over me. I didn't have time to think before he lifted me in the air. He held me by my arms. My shoulders froze. My legs dangled. He slammed me down on the bed. I landed on my tailbone. Shock waves shot up my spine. My brain went numb and tingly. My throat dried up. I wanted to cry, but I couldn't. For a moment my whole world stopped with that slam to my tailbone.

I took a painful swallow and tried to regain my composure. My whole body felt numb and there was a buzzing sound in my ears. I looked around the room and saw bright shooting stars flying across the white walls where the geckos were. Then everything turned pallid. I blinked a few times, and between the moments of black I saw Uncle Peter sitting on the bed. He calmly continued his reading:

And many false prophets shall rise, and shall
    deceive many.
And because iniquity shall abound, the love of many
    shall wax cold.
But he that shall endure unto the end, the same
    shall be saved.
And this gospel of the kingdom shall be preached in all
    the world for a witness unto all nations; and then shall
    the End come.

I said a quick prayer that he would keep reading so the lights wouldn't go out and leave me alone in the darkness with my thoughts.

■ ■

EVERY HOME HAD A DEMERIT chart. It included a table of "minors" and "majors." Minors included faults like wearing your shoes in the house or opening your eyes during prayer or stepping out of line when marching to breakfast. Majors were synonymous with vices such as disobedience, foolishness, and pride, and merited severer consequences. If any member of age—over twelve—received five majors in one day, then they qualified for special disciplinary action (SDA).

Special disciplinary actions included beatings, silence restriction, and confinement. You might be forced to confess your sins and memorize chapter upon chapter of scripture or some of Father David's letters and recite them on command. Every home had a long paddle sitting atop a high shelf. We called it "the board." Sometimes the adults drilled holes in the board so air could pass through swiftly, causing the paddle to deliver a more painful blow. Sometimes we were assigned extra house duty—scrubbing screens, mopping floors, deep-cleaning the bathrooms, or raking piles of leaves in the late afternoon. Sometimes we were put in quarantine, separated from the rest of the flock as if polluted with some childhood disease capable of spreading through the home like a virus. If we laughed or talked out of turn or mimicked someone in a mocking way, we would have to wear a wooden plank across the chest that read in bold black letters, "Please don't talk to me. I'm on silence restriction." We were forced to stay in the world of silence until instructed otherwise.

Some kids were disciplined more often than others for their rebellious nature or ornery behavior. If a child was more vocal or high-spirited than their peers, they were put into quarantine or isolated for scheduled disciplinary measures that tested their endurance. Mary Ann was beginning to develop into what the adults called a "problem child" because of her rebellious attitude and questioning nature. Tamar and I were punished often for "foolishness," but since we were twins we were sometimes punished together. Also, foolishness wasn't as serious an offense so it didn't merit as severe a consequence. This difference in treatment began to cause a rift between Mary Ann and the two of us. We were no longer "triplets," like we had been in Udon Thani. She was often being punished or in quarantine, and I could tell the pressure was beginning to take its toll. She became more withdrawn and scared and began to question the leaders.

Some of the adults, such as our group shepherds, were stricter than others, but all of them had the freedom to discipline us freely, whether or not we knew why. Uncle Paul was our group shepherd, so he was the one who disciplined us older kids, or OCs (older children). Uncle Paul had a small mouth, handsome eyes, short, stubby hair, and a cleft in his chin that made him look younger than he was. He was known to have strong arms and was one of the "strict" adults.

Some of Uncle Paul's severest punishments were reserved for his own sons. He threw them against the wall whenever they misbehaved. He grabbed them by the shoulder or by the shirt. He could pull them up from the floor just by yanking on one of their ears. If he was angry enough, he would punish two of his boys in one outburst of rage. After pulling them up from their seats and throwing them across the room, he slammed them into a wall with a startling force. Sammy, the second oldest, wore thick glasses, which he almost always lost during these bouts of punishment.

After sliding down the wall and landing on the floor, the boys picked themselves up, found the floor beneath their knees, wobbled to their feet, and stood in submission against the wall until their dad welcomed them back to class. After a while these shocking incidents became frequent occurrences, and eventually the boys became numb to their father's incongruent demonstrations of fatherly love. I always felt sorry for Sammy because not only was he hurt by the treatment, but he could barely see. After regaining his composure he'd open his eyes and squint around the room to find a sea of spectators, an audience of frightened children. He was aware that his embarrassing punishment was an example for the rest of us who might ever dare to disrespect our elders. Although I didn't always know what Uncle Paul's sons had done wrong, I always knew when one of them had acted up because their ears were bright red, even the next day.

Uncle Paul was nice to my sisters and me. He saved my life once, or at least that's how I remember it. My dad was cutting down huge stalks of sugar cane that had overgrown the swamp. I was watching, the thought of freshly squeezed cane juice stimulating the taste buds on the tip of my tongue. When the stalks were freshly cut, we'd suck them until our stomachs ached from the unfamiliar exposure to sugar. Maybe that's why I stood too close to the wild bunch of sugar cane on that particular day; I so badly wanted to taste something sweet. I remember Dad lifting the machete high into the air and then two strong hands grabbing hold of my waist, whisking me off the road faster than the stalks hit the ground. For a moment, suspended in midair, I witnessed the machete slice through the spot where I had stood a split second before.

Then one day in May 1990—three years before the Apocalypse was due to happen—five check marks appeared next to my name symbol indicating the vices disobedience, foolishness, defiance, pride, and disorderly conduct. Tamar and Mary Ann also had demerits next to their symbols. The three of us had gotten into trouble together. We'd gone wild one afternoon—the day Auntie Swiss Joy's water broke and she'd gone to the hospital with her husband and our mom to deliver her ninth child. With so few adults on duty, we acted up: playing instead of raking leaves, wearing our outside shoes in the house, laughing through mealtime, and staying up past our bedtimes. "Disorderly conduct," already a vague behavior description for a nine-year-old, could be upgraded from a minor to a major based on the supervisor's discretion, resulting in a most confusing code of ethics. I was nominated for special disciplinary action. During lunch that day I saw Mom talking to Uncle Paul. Because she was the home shepherd, I knew she had a stake in deciding the appropriate discipline for me. And since she was my mother I was certain she would never sentence me to the dreaded board. I was quieter and more withdrawn and had managed to dodge the severer forms of punishment that seemed to accrue as we kids got older.

I was told after lunch that I was scheduled for a date with Uncle Paul at two P.M. to receive the dreaded board. For her punishment, Tamar was assigned to a week of yard work during Get-Out. Mary Ann was put on silence restriction. What I had done to receive the worst sentence I'll never know. I knew there was nothing I could do to negotiate a lesser punishment. At the appointed time, Uncle Paul led me to an empty bedroom, locked the door behind him, and gave me instructions: "If you need to cry then bury your face in this pillow and try to scream quietly, please." He was holding the brown wooden paddle in his hand. The sensitivity in his voice gave me hope that maybe he would relinquish his duties. But he handed me a giant ladybug pillow, as if the synthetic red material had the power to absorb my screams. I so badly wanted for someone to hear me cry.

I clenched the railing of the top bunk.

"Wait," I said and turned to him. "Did Mom say this was okay?"

"Your mother decided this was the best course of action."

"Okay," I said. "Please can I keep my pants on?" I was begging now.

"You can keep your pants on," he replied, his voice still soft and tender.

I was wearing my sapphire-blue shorts with greasy oil stains from the time I hoarded deep-fried bananas in my pockets and forgot to eat them. (Anything made with grease or sugar was a treat and worth the risk to hoard even if it left stains in the only pair of shorts I owned.) The thin cotton material provided minimal cushioning for my already well-padded bottom, so it didn't matter if I was unclothed or not; it was going to hurt anyway.

Over time we kids had developed a technique to prepare for contact during paddling and make the impact of the blows less painful. We preferred standing. I closed my eyes, shrugged my shoulders to my ears, and held my breath. Then I tightened my buttocks and locked my knees. I squeezed my butt cheeks as hard as possible till they were firm as a board, then found any stable object nearby to grasp, as if holding on could make me let go.

I turned my head to him and mumbled, "Can you try to get both sides?" My lower lip quivered.

"What?" He hadn't heard my request.

"It's just that I want it to be even, so can you try to hit both sides, not just one?" I said, trying to hold back the tears, but to no avail.

"I'll try my best."

Uncle Paul never looked me in the eye. He held his head low, so low that I could see the little spot on the top of his head that was starting to bald.

I prepared myself for the first swing in hopes that maybe if he struck me hard enough then my whole backside would go numb and I wouldn't be able to feel the rest of the punishment. Or, better yet, the pain would shoot up the nerves of my spine and cause a state of delirium in my brain, resulting in an unconscious state in which my body would be liberated from pain and my mind free of fear. My plan of escape didn't work. Instead, I managed to dodge the first strike. Now Uncle Paul was mad. He shook his head in disappointment. He let out a sigh of frustration and took hold of my arm. He positioned me back into place.

"If you don't cooperate then I'll have to take drastic measures," he said. This time his voice was stern. I knew what he was capable of. "Now let's do this quick and get it over with." Then he said what Dad always said before he disciplined us: "This is going to hurt me more than it hurts you." I didn't mind much when Dad spanked or disciplined us, but I knew this was going to be much worse.

I again grabbed the bunk bed railing, my fingernails digging into the splinters of the unfinished wood. I closed my eyes and buried my face in the oversized ladybug pillow. I prepared again for contact by locking my knees and squeezing my butt cheeks. With my eyes closed, I let out a silent prayer. If God could ever have granted me a chance to escape the agony of feeling, I would have taken it then, but looking back on my life I've learned that the moments when I wished I could escape were the moments that made me stronger. If I knew what I had done wrong, then I would have sent out a request for forgiveness. But I could never be sorry for being a child.

Each of the seven strikes sent me into a deeper state of delirium.

"Please stop!" I begged.

"Into the pillow," he said. I felt my knees get weak. Soon I had to hold on to the railing as my legs gave way underneath me.

■ ■

THAT NIGHT DAD CAME TO my bedside. He sat down and ran his hands through my hair.

"Don't cry, babes," he said. "Your tears are so salty." He took his thumb and ran it down my tear-stained cheeks.

"You see your sister over there?" he pointed to a bed nearby where Tamar lay with her back toward me, her little body shivering, "She's crying too."

"Why, Daddy? She didn't even get a spanking."

"She's crying for you, babes. She thinks you're dying a slow, painful death."

"Is that what she told you?"

"Yes."

On other nights I cried myself to sleep because I was never going to live to see adulthood *and* I was going to die a martyr. But this night was different. I was crying because I had been punished by a person I thought I could trust. I was punished by the man who was supposed to protect me, the man I thought was my hero, the man who kissed me good night on the cheek every night, my replacement for Dad.

I was beginning to see that the adults, Mom and Dad included, would take whatever measures necessary to keep us in line and loyal to Father David's teachings. I began to withdraw further and further inside myself, unable to handle both the fear of death that was always with me and now my recognition of what the adults were turning into.

I stopped crying that night, just to relieve Tamar of her tears.

CHAPTER 21

FATHER DAVID WARNED AGAINST THE dangers of becoming "blobs." In groups, we could become stagnant and complacent. We were always on the move. "Modern-day gypsies" Father David called us, and he was Abraham the Gypsy King, one of the characters from his fictional Spirit World, where everyone gets murdered for God in the end. When it was time to flee, we once again packed our things in large black garbage bags and found refuge at our next destination.

One morning a few weeks after my punishment the leaders announced during breakfast that the Phuket home would be closing. The landlord needed the property cleared for renovations. The leaders in central headquarters had found homes for all of us to relocate to: Shem and Joy would be moving to Songkhla, located on the southern coast, to open a new home there. We were headed to the town of Hat Yai, which neighbored Songkhla. Uncle French John and Auntie Meekness would live in Bangkok, in an already established home, and Uncle Paul and Auntie Mary moved to the Philippines, where Auntie Mary was from. The night before we left, Tamar and I sat in a bottom bunk bed trying to tally up how many places we'd lived.

"Do you want to count countries or continents?" Tamar said.

"Let's count cities," I said.

After a while, we lost count.

"Do you think we'll ever find a real home to stay in for a long time?" I asked Tamar, who was lying down, staring at a poster of heaven that had been tacked to the underside of the top bunk's wooden frame.

"Probably not," she said. She was running her fingers along the poster's white borders.

"It's okay," I said. "As long as we can stay together and don't have to be separated from Mom and Dad forever."

We stayed at the home in Hat Yai for a few months before relocating to Songkhla. Besides Shem and Joy, a few other families lived in the home there, including Paul and Felicity, who had just arrived from India with their five children. The day after we left Hat Yai, a flood hit the area and wiped out whole villages. The waters rose eight feet high and swept cars away. People rushed to the rooftops of their houses. In photos of Dad and Mom visiting the village after the flood, they are sitting in a *tuk-tuk*. Mom is holding Becky, and the water comes clear up to the top of the wheels. I heard a woman recounting in Thai the story of the flood. She gestured with her hands to a grey mark on the wall about two feet above her head, indicating where the waters had risen.

Now we could add a flood to the list of things we had fled. I wasn't sure if the flood was the enemy's doing or God's. I didn't bother trying too hard to figure it out.

■ ■

OUR HOME IN SONGKHLA WAS different from the ones in Phuket and Hat Yai. It was bigger, with a large, spacious dining room and more bedrooms that held rows of bunk beds and trundle beds. As with all our homes, it was protected by high walls and boarded gates, and it resided on the outskirts of town rather than in the city so we wouldn't be conspicuous. A large backyard was covered with gravel, and a small pond housed batches of tadpoles and newly developed frogs. I couldn't wait to play with them. Because we were close to fishing ports, a faint smell of fish and salt lingered in the air. When we arrived, Uncle Dutch Sam, the home cook, was out back unloading a large barracuda that looked like a miniature shark, with jagged teeth and glassy, ferocious eyes. I looked closely and noticed that its eyes were frozen open and its body full of icy scales. "Look what the Lord provided," Uncle Sam said. He said he had obtained the fish from the nearby harbor on provisioning day. "Enough fish to feed us for days." But it was so ugly and mean looking. I didn't want a bite of it.

Along with "provisioning" as a means of income, the Family continued worldwide distribution (for donations) of tapes, videos, newsletters, and other promotional materials that had been produced at the home in Japan. "Witnessing" (for money) also became a more important source of income. When I was young, children hadn't been expected to spend much time in the outside world; that was a job for adults. But now we were required to accompany our parents and the shepherds on their witnessing trips, performing on the streets, singing songs about God, and

asking for donations. We weren't supposed to think of our performances as begging, but along with video sales they had become a
main source of income.

On the occasions when I went out witnessing, I saw that
Songkhla, a fishing village close to the Malaysian border, boasted
the kind of nightlife you would find in the tourist hotspot of
Phuket. Christmas-colored neon lights flashed words in English:
"Nude Dancers," "All-Night Karaoke," "Special Thai Massage."
American Navy officers, drunk and belligerent and looking for
a good time, wore shiny silver badges and gold tassels and held
young Thai girls on their arms. When money got tight we dressed
in frilly pink dresses and went to the harbor to sing about God's
love and salvation. Our aim was to collect donations from the
seamen who made their living on the ships that landed there. Our
costumes were sewn by one of the Thai aunties. They were of a
simple design, and you could tell that the material came from one
long roll of cloth. Seven or eight of us gathered in the living room
the night before to practice singing in sync. I didn't have much of
a singing voice.

We took *tuk-tuks* or *song-taows* to our destination—often it was
the harbor, but sometimes it was a nearby rural or coastal neighborhood. Mom came with us. Even though she was pregnant
again she was still able to catch a glance from the seamen when
we sang on the ships. Sometimes they tried to touch her. "They
must be desperate," she'd say, "trying to flirt with a big pregnant
lady like me." Even though the days of flirty-fishing were over,
Father David encouraged women to use their eyes to tell lonely
men about God's love. "The look of love," he called it. I was nine
years old.

The harbor bustled with excitement. Large box crates were
transferred from ship to dock. Oversized cranes rearranged the
containers after they landed. Ships coming in and going out

blared their horns. The best part was hearing the burly men give commands in a language I could understand. "That crate goes here." "Load the dock." "Aye aye, Captain!" At the harbor, even though I was outside the walls, I was no longer a foreigner.

Once onboard the ship, we went from cabin to cabin and sang:

I wanna share my love with you,
And all you gotta do,
Is say you want me to,
To share my love with you.

In unison, we gestured open palm to heart and then out to the audience of mostly men, as if to spread God's love generously to anyone who was willing to receive it.

There is no love like mine,
No matter where in the world you go.
The world can't satisfy,
The hunger that you feel inside.

Sometimes the sailors gifted us with souvenirs from their native lands, and we would accept them, allowing the men to wrap their arms around us and pull us in for a hug or a kiss on the cheek. When it was late we walked through the passageways and saw prostitutes with heavy makeup, long black hair, and garments made of Thai silk talking lovingly to the bearded men. The prostitutes on the ships were different from the ones on the streets. Their skirts dangled past their ankles, just high enough to reveal their painted red toenails peeking out from silver sandal straps. Their hair was pulled into tight buns or ponytails. Their colorful makeup was blended evenly with their milky skin tone, not worn thick and splotchy like that of the street girls. They laughed and giggled in timid voices, covering their bright pink lips with their delicate hands and long, waving fingers. Their hair smelled of gardenia, and they left an aura of jasmine perfume that seemed to linger long after they walked through the passageways.

When we drove home in the evenings, we were encouraged to count the lost souls we'd saved for the day along with any baht we'd collected from tape and video distribution. The van shook every time the tires hit a hole in the road. The sky would be brilliant with stars. "Hallelujah! Thank You, Jesus! What a wonderful day out witnessing!" the auntie said, her long brown hair hanging down over her flower-print dress.

"How many souls did we win today to God's Heavenly Kingdom? Hallelujah." I would rack my brain for some numerical answer. Every soul won was an extra star on our crown when we sat with King Jesus for the Marriage Supper of the Lamb, our upcoming first dinner in heaven.

Late one night, after we'd finished singing our set and offered the seamen posters, asking if they knew Jesus, a brawny Russian named Boris asked me if I had ever seen a deep freezer before. The other kids were there too, but he seemed to take an interest in me. He wore a plaid shirt with jeans and suspenders. He had a scruffy beard, small smiling eyes, and hairy knuckles.

"No," I replied.

"Have you ever lived in cold weather?" he asked.

I shook my head. Sweden didn't count because I was a baby when we left so I didn't remember it.

"Wanna feel cold?" he continued. Before I had time to answer, he hoisted me over the metal rail above a massive deep freezer the size of a basketball court. Suspended in midair, my feet dangled above the icy hollow below. The air curled like steam from walls of ice. Men looking like ants dressed in black snowsuits were packing fish and loading meat. I knew it was a heck of a fall to the bottom.

If he dropped me I would splatter to my death on the rocky sheets of ice below. I hoped he wouldn't let go of me. Mom was busy witnessing to a couple of men eager to hear God's message, and I wondered if she knew what this man was doing to me.

Later that evening when we were counting the souls we'd won, I whispered to Tamar that I wasn't sure I'd won any.

"What about Boris?" she said. I had told her about him.

Guiltily, I remembered that in the middle of my harrowing experience dangling above a giant deep freezer, I may have forgotten to ask Boris to receive Jesus Christ into his heart as his Lord and Savior.

CHAPTER 22

IN LATE OCTOBER 1993, MY siblings and I were summoned to a private meeting with our parents. I was twelve. I had begun to wonder if maybe the Apocalypse that Father David had predicted wasn't going to come. Maybe I was going to live to be an adult. I had started puberty, and my concern over the changing shape of my body had displaced concerns about my death. Plus, the sequence of events narrated in the book of Revelation hadn't unfolded as foretold: the Antichrist hadn't risen to power, there was no "one world government" or "one world order," and we hadn't heard anything about the mark of the beast or the Great Tribulation.

"Father David had a revelation from God," Dad said calmly

once we were seated in a circle on the floor. "And it looks like it's time for us to move back to the West."

I thought about Father David's letters about America from the early days. America was a whore, Father David said—a spiritual cesspool. I remembered the cartoon of a sharp-boned woman representing the country. She sat with her legs spread wide, pearl necklaces splayed across her neck, holding the U.S. Capitol building in one hand and an overflowing bowl of jewels and riches in the other. In the distance sat an image of an Egyptian pyramid next to a swaying palm tree. Large block letters read, "Babylon the Great Whore: Get Out of Her Before She Gets You!" Father David called American capitalism "spiritual fornication" and spoke of how "she will sell you into a drunken stupor of job slavery, idol-making, bloodshed, and dollar worship." People in the United States were ignorant, and it was our job to save them. The Western world was finally ready to hear our message.

"Are we going to live in Sweden?" Mary Ann said. "I wanna live in snow! Don't you have family there, Mommy?"

"Yes," Mom said. "But that's not for us to decide. We have to see what's in God's highest will."

"Why are we moving back West?" Tamar asked. "I thought the West was evil. Isn't that what Grandpa says?"

"Well, it's a little hard to explain," Dad said. "But Father David said Western nations need to hear our message too. This is their final opportunity to repent."

"Before the Great Apocalypse?" Tamar asked. "Does that mean we have more time?"

Father David wrote that God had given us an extension because he was pleased with our work. Still, I wondered why we were moving back to the West now. Why hadn't we just stayed there when we were young?

"A small home in the suburbs of Chicago has room for us," Dad said. "So we'll be living in America soon."

The idea was exhilarating.

"Yay!" Tamar exclaimed gleefully. "We get to go on a plane ride again!"

Soon, I was as excited as Tamar and had forgotten all about Father David's illustration of America the Babylon Whore. Even though I had lived in some of the most beautiful places on Earth, I was very intrigued to hear that America would be my new home. But most of all I was excited that I would be together with my family on a long plane ride across the ocean.

■ ■

I KNEW THAT THE AMERICA Dad was from was far from the America we were destined for. I looked up detailed pictures in the encyclopedia. Chicago would be much colder than California. It would have real seasons, when trees turned vibrant red or golden. This America would have sprawling suburbs and fenced neighborhoods with manicured lawns, and clustered epicenters where important people conducted important business in important business suits. This America was home to one of the tallest buildings in the world (the magnificent Sears Tower), sat on the banks of one of the largest lakes in the world (Lake Michigan), and was much colder than the Thai beaches where we swam. This America was foreign and exotic compared to the life I knew in Thailand.

I didn't know whether Chicago was a city or a state. Mom cleared up the confusion, and soon I could locate the Windy City on any map of the world, even a large globe.

I had heard stories about America—stories of Father David traveling on his evangelical missions with his mother and attending grade school at Comstock in Oklahoma, where he was bullied and started speaking to God in the solitude of nature. Stories of the early days of the Children of God, when young hippies gathered in parks and on piers to rebel against the government and stage protests against the mainstream church so they could find purpose and meaning in their lives by serving God. America was evil. America was the whore. Although I had lived there briefly as a child, America seemed like a forbidden pleasure, and now the succulent temptation sparkled within reach. I felt impure at merely the thought of freedom. I was Eve in the Garden of Eden, tempted to take a bite, and finally the fruit was at my fingertips and ripe for picking. People in America spoke my language. People in America wore jeans. People in America were cool. I couldn't stop thinking, *My life is about to change forever.* . . .

■ ■

FIRST TASK—SHOPPING. MOM TOLD US we had to look nice. "People in America are different," she said. I wondered if I would feel like a foreigner no matter where I lived. A few weeks before we were scheduled to leave, Mom selected me to represent my sisters and accompany her on an exclusive shopping trip to prepare us for America.

I had never been shopping before. All my life everything I owned had fit neatly into a small pink basket the size of a large encyclopedia volume. The only other time I had spent money was earlier that year. One month we had a surplus in our budget after rent was paid, and each child in the home was given thirty-two baht, the equivalent of one dollar, to spend how we wanted. We were told to turn in our money along with our request before the weekly shopping trip to the local market. I requested a pen. It was my very first pen. The metal point curved inward, making it difficult to write with, but I never planned to use it anyway. I don't know what prompted me to buy it, because even though I knew how to read and write, I wasn't allowed to do either on my own unless it pertained to Father David's teachings or I was being supervised by a shepherd. But the pen remained a token to me. It meant somewhere deep inside I had a passion. I was somebody. I kept the pen for a very long time, but I never used it.

Shopping for clothes didn't carry as much significance as my red tip pen, but the task presented a whole new set of challenges. I had never cared about my outward appearance. We wore hand-me-downs. Father David said any type of style sense was of the devil. Women were not allowed to wear makeup and had to grow their hair long and keep it unstyled. Men were required to keep clean-shaven with short hair. Jeans and logos of any kind were forbidden. My wardrobe consisted of a couple of tank tops (we called them "singlets"), a few pairs of shorts, underwear, and flip-flops.

As we browsed through the market, clothes hanging above the entryways whipped across my head every time I entered a stall, reminding me I was tall. Mom grabbed my arm and tugged me close, telling me I was beautiful. She had a way of making me feel as if I were in grave danger whenever I was out in public places.

Once in the changing room I slipped into my first pair of jeans. The back pocket read Levi's. The bulky material gripped every inch of my awkwardly shifting hips. I had never felt so constrained in my entire life, as if the jeans could trap any freedom in my body. I tugged at the zipper and forced the button into its hole. The hems stopped just short of my ankles. On my next exhalation, my breath constricted and shifted rapidly from the depths of my lower belly to the upper part of my chest. I stepped out of the changing room and eyed myself in a full-length mirror. I was cool and hip and ready to face America.

Next I found the perfect shirt, silky and smooth, with a neat collar and pearly pink buttons. I chose pink for me since I was girly, yellow for Mary Ann since her hair was blonde, and orange for Tamar since orange went well with pink, I thought.

Finding shoes that fit our large-boned Scandinavian feet was always a challenge in Thailand, but this task was particularly daunting. First, I must find the perfect fit. Second, I must look good. Suddenly, with the prospect of living in America, I was keenly aware of my outer image, and for the first time in my life I felt self-conscious.

Mom suggested we wear closed-toed shoes for the plane ride since planes were "dirty." I found the perfect pair of men's loafers, a size eight, solid brown with tassels. Tamar's were dark blue, one size larger, minus the tassels, but equally ugly.

■ ■

IT TOOK DAD AND JOHN six months to raise the money we needed to buy thirteen tickets: four thousand dollars. It seemed like a lot of money. I had never seen real money before and had no idea what that amount would look like, but I knew it must have been a huge stack. Every day they left early in the morning and came home late. One night after everyone had gone to bed, I stood at the doorway of my room and watched Dad walk up the stairs after a long day of witnessing. His white cotton dress shirt was half unbuttoned. He held his head low and dragged his feet. He looked tired and hungry. I knew what those outings were like. He had spent the whole day at the harbor going from ship to ship, witnessing to the sailing men, offering tapes and videos in exchange for a suggested donation. When the girls went on witnessing excursions, we wore short skirts or pink dresses with ruffles and lace. I watched Dad in his exhaustion and then tiptoed back to bed, excited and anxious about what lay ahead.

The evening before our departure I paced under the shade of a mango tree. I had heard about teens in the Western world. We knew about the "walkout" from Father David's and Mama Maria's letters. (Mama Maria was entrusted with writing some letters starting shortly after Davidito was born.) She informed us that after a push to move our mission to Europe, hundreds of second-generation teens there had staged a walkout. Father David said they had become polluted and had succumbed to the temptations of the world after their first taste of modernism and worldliness. Some committed suicide not long after. I was warned that if I left the Family I would be susceptible to a similar fate.

The night before we left, Mom invited us to her room and laid out our options for clothing. We each had been given two sweaters. For us girls, one was yellowish-brown with smudges of lotus flowers, and the other was navy blue with smaller flowers and less fuzz. Each was wrapped in crisp cellophane. We didn't have money to buy winter clothes, so someone had donated the big, furry sweaters to our family. It was mid-April, and we had been warned about the chill factor in Chicago that made fifty degrees feel like thirty. A simple breeze could make you feel like you were being poked by a thousand needles. One sweater was to wear on the flight since the airplane would be cold. Mom suggested that we wear the brown one. It was oversized and scratchy and was lined with a stiff linen that made me feel as if I were wrapped in a package when I wore it.

We were each given a "flee bag" for our move—matching small black suitcases—with a padlock and two silver keys. It was the very first time I'd owned anything of significant value—my very own suitcase. In my back right pocket I carried the tiny keys, which were linked together by a sinewy piece of thread. Small as the suitcase was, I wasn't quite sure how I was going to fill the whole thing. Luckily, the extra sweater bundled up into the perfect suitcase stuffer.

I took out my glittery lock, shiny and precious and green. I planned to keep the key close to me during the long flight. I had nothing to protect, yet I felt secure knowing that soon I would be living in a first-world country, where the streets were clean and the water was safe to drink from the tap, where cockroaches and rats didn't roam freely. I would be alone with my family for a very long time on a plane ride that would carry me across the Pacific Ocean.

Everything was going to be okay. I would be living in America soon, where people spoke my language and I wouldn't be a foreigner anymore.

■ ■

WE STOPPED IN KOREA FOR a layover and took photos at the airport. John was wearing the tightest black corduroy pants I had ever seen. His psychedelic shirt was bright green with yellow paisleys. He wore it tucked in and buttoned up all the way. His hair was slicked back into a wavy style that didn't budge, as if the individual hairs had been super-glued to one another. I wondered where he got the hair gel since no members were allowed to style their hair. He reminded me of John Travolta in *Grease,* one of the movies on our Recommended List. He was starting to look like one of the "cool kids" in Father David's comic books. Was he being influenced in a worldly way because he was getting older and we were moving to America? Was he like some of the teens in Europe we had heard about? Was he becoming a systemite?

The flight lasted eighteen hours. There was a big-screen TV above the center row a few seats ahead of us. We watched movies that were not on the Recommended List. I didn't feel guilty. A stewardess approached, her heels clicking lightly on the narrow walkway. "You all must be brothers and sisters. So beautiful and well-behaved." She wore bright-pink lipstick and had her hair pulled back in a tight bun. She was smacking gum so loudly I almost couldn't understand what she said.

She handed us peanuts in bright packages that read "honey roasted." I had never tasted anything so sweet and crunchy. Even though Father David preached about the damaging health effects of eating sugar, I didn't feel guilty. The stewardess gave us each a glittery bouncing ball, a reel of colorful stickers, and a small Korean Air aircraft souvenir. Still no guilt. On that plane ride I began to wonder how harmful the sparkling temptations of the outside world really were.

CHAPTER 23

WHEN I STEPPED ACROSS THE narrow gap between aircraft and bridgeway, a sharp chill shot straight to my bones. I inhaled the flavor of fresh, crisp air. The dryness stung my lungs, piercing every lobe. For a split second the wind overtook me, and I blinked back the bitter cold. We had arrived in America.

Inside the airport, enormous windows looked out over the tarmac; the high, domed ceilings let in natural sunlight. People walked briskly, as if they had somewhere important to go, dragging their rolling suitcases on bright, polished floors. I had never seen so many white people in one place. They appeared tiny against the grandiosity of the airport.

Dad went to make a phone call. We waited for him next to an elaborate perfume store displaying "Duty Free" signs and numerous boxes of elegant perfume bottles wrapped in shiny, delicate packages. Nearby, I overheard two men dressed in crisp business suits: "Hey, man. How'd your trip go?"

"It went great."

"You here on business or pleasure?"

"Both, man."

"That's great. Wanna grab a drink while we wait?" They looked like they had stepped straight out of the America I'd read about in the encyclopedia.

In Thailand, my family had been a sight to behold. People stopped to stare. They'd count us and feed us and touch our skin and marvel at the sight of twins. Some thought that Mary Ann, Tamar, and I were triplets, or quadruplets with Heidi. They'd shout their awe over a loudspeaker at a crowded market or festival. But here we received no such attention. We passed through customs smoothly, telling the officials, as we had on visa trips, that we were Swedish and Dad was an English teacher. I claimed my suitcase stuffed with my giant furry sweater. I still carried the silver key in my pocket. Outside, we met Uncle Tim, the home shepherd, and squeezed into a taxi plus a van.

The freeways were smooth and uncluttered, much different from the bumpy dirt roads in Udon Thani and the crammed highways in Bangkok. Everything was silent. The cars stayed in their lanes and used turn signals when exiting or maneuvering. There was no cacophony of horns honking or motorbikes racing by.

I kept turning my head, looking out the windows for the America I'd read about. It was clean and pristine, just like I'd imagined it would be. When I breathed in, the sharp air stung my nostrils and chilled my nose, but the van was warm and cozy, silent aside from the low humming of the engine. The silence was precise and made my ears ring. A strange calm washed over me. My body relaxed and my limbs felt lighter, like they'd been deflated. I was excited that we were moving to America instead of Sweden, which, according to the encyclopedias, was cold and sparsely populated. America was exciting, the center of "cool," and the forbidden place Father David had warned us about. I felt lucky to be moving back, and I wondered how long we'd stay this time.

We drove past elegant buildings that towered above the roads encircling them. I spelled out signs in a language I could understand: "off ramp," "exit," "O'Hare Airport." Street names sounded Hollywood-movie prestigious: 3rd Street, Taylor Drive, Pulaski Avenue. I could tell by the overpasses and underpasses and fancy looping highway structures and smooth, shiny cars that this was a much grander system than the world I knew in Thailand.

As we neared our new neighborhood in Berwyn, a middle-class suburb south of Chicago, all the houses looked the same: three identical stories with rectangular windows, and steps descending from the front door to a lawn surrounded by a fence. Every few blocks we passed a park that featured elaborate, colorful play gyms with metal bars and wood chips covering the ground. A soft snow melted that day.

"Can we touch it?" Becky, who had just turned five, asked. "I wanna build a snowman!"

"Winter is almost over," Mom said. "But I'm sure we can still try to build a snowman with the leftover snow." She sounded excited, and I wondered if the snow brought back memories from her youth in Sweden.

Our home, located on South Oak Park between 16th and 18th Streets, was a three-story brick unit overlooking sidewalks bordered by manicured lawns planted with low oak trees and tall, elegant pines. Mom said we were lucky to find such a nice home in an affluent neighborhood for cheap rent. I was excited to explore.

There was a sharp chill in the air, but the house was warm, with heaters humming in almost every corner.

"You're just in time for breakfast," a woman who introduced herself as Auntie Faithy said. "It'll be a very late breakfast, but that's okay. The house rules here in the U.S. aren't as strict." She wore thick glasses and an apron with frilly ruffles around her heavy waist.

"They're called 'bay-gulls,'" she said as she brought over a steaming tray of bright-green, oversized bread rolls. "They were a donation from the bagel shop down the street."

I had never heard of a "bay-gull" or a "bagel shop." They were green because they were leftovers from St. Patrick's Day. We'd never heard of St. Patrick's Day either, although Dad was part Irish. It was a systemite celebration.

On a small white plate next to the bagels sat a perfect block of cold, hard butter under a fancy glass lid. There were butter knives, which were foreign to us and seemed an unnecessary invention. I had never seen real butter before. It melted in my mouth. The bagels, despite their fluorescent-green color, gave me my first experience of white-flour delight. Auntie Faithy brought over a plate of fried eggs that glistened like thick layers of silk. Unlike the powdered eggs I was used to forcing down, the fried egg slid down my throat effortlessly. To my delight, I was allowed seconds. For the first time in my life I wasn't just full; I was satisfied.

We met our new housemates: Tim and Joy, who were Canadian and had recently arrived from India with their nine kids; single-mom Christina and her five kids; Faithy and her daughter; and a few young adults and teen girls. Christina was from a family who had been Dad's neighbors in California when he was younger.

"During the day we keep the curtains closed and the windows and doors shut," Auntie Faithy said as she cleared our breakfast plates from the table. She turned to look at us as she neared the kitchen, which was separated from the dining room by an open countertop. "We wouldn't want anyone knowing how many people live in this house."

The landlords were an old Italian couple who wouldn't be checking on the building, so they wouldn't know how many people lived here either. The house had three bedrooms plus a basement and an attic that had been turned into sleeping quarters. They contained so many beds there was almost no place to walk. Tamar and I met Michelle, Christina's second-eldest daughter, who was a year younger than we were. She introduced us to Sam, Tim and Joy's oldest son, who was cute, with sandy blond hair and dreamy eyes. They were as excited to have fresh faces in their home as we were to meet them. They wanted to hear about life in Thailand, but we were so tired we passed out immediately after breakfast on a mattress on the floor in the attic.

When we woke up, Sam and Michelle were laughing at us. Tamar and I lay in identical positions, with one arm covering our eyes and one knee bent, just the way you'd imagine twins would sleep. Our new friends found it hilarious.

■ ■

THE FIRST DIFFERENCE I NOTICED about life in America was that there were no high walls around our home. A chain-link fence that reached to my waist surrounded our house—the only protection we had. We still had to keep hidden behind closed curtains. The second thing I noticed was the plentiful food. When we awoke the first morning, we found on the table a bowl of oranges with skin that seemed as thick as watermelon rind and the sweetest-smelling juice that squirted into our eyes when we peeled them if we weren't careful. We were allowed to eat even if it wasn't mealtime—even if we weren't hungry!

Auntie Faithy was right when she said the rules were more relaxed. In the afternoon we watched TV, which wasn't supposed to be allowed in the Family. It was my first time watching television. The 1994 Winter Olympics, something else I'd never been exposed to, were on. The Nancy Kerrigan and Tonya Harding scandal was making headline news. Over and over I watched the clip of Nancy Kerrigan wailing in pain, holding her knee after some men hired by Tonya Harding had bashed it with a crowbar in the locker room. I couldn't help but notice the beauty of the sport. When the skaters glided across the ice, they looked happy and free. And they were *beautiful*. I watched as sixteen-year-old Ukrainian Oksana Baiul upset the competition and won gold. I wanted to rejoice with her. I wanted to *be* her. I couldn't help thinking, *Sports can't be evil.* Father David had taught us that all sports—along with movies, education, and a normal day job— were evil.

It was in Berwyn that I developed my first real crush. In the basement we had free access to a large, bulky computer. The Family had recently begun receiving computers as donations from sponsors and using them for correspondence and for keeping track of witnessing data and publications. But the computer also had a few games on it. I learned a game in which words floated down the screen and exploded like bombs if I could type them correctly in time.

One day while playing I turned around to find Sam standing behind me. When I stood up we were so close together that I could feel his breath on my lips. He put his hands around my waist and pulled me closer. I liked the way he made me feel. I noticed an unfamiliar heat in my body. My pulse raced.

"Have you ever done this before?" he whispered, and I could almost feel his lips against mine.

As badly as I wanted to kiss him, I pulled away and ran upstairs.

■ ■

THERE WERE OTHER RITES OF passage. In Thailand we kids understood humiliation, but only as a form of punishment inflicted by our parents and shepherds with Father David's approval. Although Tamar, Mary Ann, and I had sometimes bullied other girls who were weaker than us, I'd never been humiliated by my peers, especially for being different. Since my dad was from the United States, it never occurred to me that I wasn't "American" and that I would have to adjust to a new and completely different culture. But we stood out more in the U.S. than we had in Thailand.

It was much more difficult keep a low profile without high walls. We tried to blend in when we left the house on our daily walks to the park to play on the elaborate jungle gyms. But we could only blend in so much. We traded sweaters each day, sometimes wearing one on top of the other so we looked like giant stuffed teddy bears waddling through the neighborhood. One day somebody accidently poured bleach into the washer and stained our pants. They came out of the dryer with white splotches all over the legs. They were one of only two pairs of jeans I owned. A group of young girls spotted us in the park.

"Hey," the ringleader said, "are you guys homeless or something?"

We kept swinging on our swings and kicking up the wood chips as if it were nothing.

"Why don't you answer us? Are you guys mute or something?" the girl said.

They began yelling out unfamiliar names, such as "bitch" and "cocksucker." They continued to make fun of how we were dressed. We didn't answer until Michelle, our newfound friend, told them to back off and that we had just arrived from Thailand. She said, "*And* they are missionaries."

They started laughing hard. It stung me in a way I hadn't felt before. I knew I was the butt of their joke. I wasn't aware that another person could make me feel ugly and worthless. That day I learned they could. I was beginning to see that trying to fit in here was going to be a much bigger challenge than I had anticipated.

■ ■

FATHER DAVID HAD ENCOURAGED US in one of his letters to reach out to churches and people of other cultures so that we could blend in and also could receive help. After we performed at an Asian cultural festival, a man named Mr. Pongsak approached us. He was impressed that this white family could sing in Thai with nearly perfect accents.

"I'm the pastor of St. Paul Thai Lutheran Community Church in Forest Park," he said to Mom and Dad. He had a familiar Thai accent.

"Most of the congregation is Thai," he said. "You are welcome to attend the sermon every week on Sundays, and Wednesday evenings too. We serve a free lunch. Authentic Thai food." Since we could sing in Thai we could perform for his church, he said. "And you are lucky. The whole congregation can speak English very well." He smiled warmly.

We began attending Sunday services. I discovered I felt more at home around Thai people than I did around Americans. The congregation readily adopted us into their parish. Mr. Pongsak had a feminine face with slanted eyes, a wide jaw, and soft lips. He always wore rectangular glasses and combed his hair neatly to the side; I never saw him wear any other color than black. On sermon days he wore a cloak with a little white strip down the center of his throat. He spoke in Thai, but for our benefit the church provided an interpreter for the entire sermon.

Father David was right that churches were generous. The best part was that if we sat through the whole sermon, we enjoyed the most delicious buffet, including Thai dishes that were unfamiliar to me—pad thai, fried rice, chicken curry, spring egg rolls, chili beef stir-fry, and sweet coconut desserts.

■ ■

IN THE FALL WE VISITED the arboretum, where I was awed by the brilliance of the autumn colors—fiery orange oak trees, low shrubs illuminated with the brightest tones of pink and yellow and green, golden willows that danced over a lake whose surface seemed as still as ice. Ducks waded by with their heads high, as if to forewarn a brutal winter ahead. I tasted apple cider, warm and comforting and spiced with cinnamon.

Once I hit puberty, with my mind preoccupied by my maturing body rather than by worries of death, and now with no high walls to confine me, I began to experience the world through my senses. America was full of color, and I experienced nature in a way I hadn't in tropical Thailand. I was enchanted by the seductive hues of fall. In winter the icicles shimmered on naked branches, reflecting the glistening sun after the rain froze unexpectedly overnight. I witnessed the first blanket of snow that softened the sidewalk and announced the arrival of winter. Christmas fruitcake, loaded with tiny raisins and candied cranberries, was soft and spongy. I'd never lived through a change of seasons. Dad always said Thailand had three seasons: "Hot, super hot, and damn hot!"

Considering that the world hadn't ended and we were closing in on 1994, Father David began to admit in his letters that he might have been a bit off in his apocalyptic predictions. We kids didn't talk much about this fact; we were more concerned with our social obligations and the new world we were discovering.

Still, I found myself wondering, *Is there any truth to anything Father David said?*

One day I saw a stack of letters sitting on the kitchen counter. There were the familiar *Good News* newsletters, along with monthly prayer requests and announcements. I noticed one I had never seen before. Its black and white cover displayed a picture of Jesus strapped to a white horse and surrounded by billowing clouds. He was galloping down to Earth from heaven. A headline in bold letters read, "It Could Happen This Year."

I was beginning to have my doubts about the Children of God, but it would be years before I dared to express them.

CHAPTER 24

IT WAS THE MORNING OF February 15, 1995. Every year the adults fasted and prayed for three days leading up to Father David's birthday on February 18. We kids ate yogurt with fruit and nuts for breakfast and lunch, and soup or steamed vegetables for dinner. On the fourth day we broke the fast with a feast and celebration. This year we were told there would be a special announcement after breakfast. I noticed that some of the adults, the home shepherds in particular, had been acting a bit differently over the past few days, somber and pensive, as though their minds were elsewhere. The air was abuzz with electricity, and there was a rumor that Father David was finally going to reveal his face to us.

Tamar and I sat close together and fiddled with each other's dress hems. The night before, the adults had gathered for a special meeting that went late into the night. I wondered if maybe they'd been let in on news we weren't supposed to hear.

"What do you think he's gonna say this time?" Tamar whispered.

"I don't know," I said. There was no telling what kind of revelation Father David would conjure up. Meetings could sometimes go on for hours. Outside, a light snow had begun to fall.

Then the words I never expected to hear echoed through the living room: "Grandpa, our beloved Father in the Lord, has gone to be with Jesus."

There was a moment of silence so sharp I could almost hear the fresh snowflakes settling on the sidewalk outside. The adults broke into weeping.

Uncle Tim, the home shepherd said, "Father David is dead." His words fell like a sudden crack in the Earth's surface.

Father David had been the heartbeat of the Children of God. I had been taught to love and honor reverently even though I never knew him. He was the force that had kept the Children of God alive. He plotted our every move and dictated exactly how we would live until the Great Apocalypse of 1993. What was going to happen next? He had been the mouthpiece of God. Life without him would be like life without air. This was a death I *wasn't* prepared for.

"Does anyone have any questions?" Uncle Tim said.

I glanced at Mom and Dad. Mom, whom I'd seen cry many times, had tears streaming down her face. I couldn't tell if Dad had tears in his eyes. One of the women started weeping hysterically and speaking in tongues and saying, "Jesus, Jesus, Jesus" over and over again. Some of the other adults were holding each other, rocking back and forth, and praying desperately, like they did when they rebuked the enemy or cast out our deadly sins. Others looked euphoric, like they did after hours of praying and singing, as though they'd been transported to another world, no longer burdened with earthly concerns.

Someone asked how he died. Apparently, it was from a case of shingles, but he'd had digestive problems, too. One of his letters revealed that he may have had esophageal issues, possibly cancer. But he never went to a doctor (because he didn't believe in them), so his illness worsened. I'd never known anyone with cancer.

The adults broke into muffled praises and continued speaking in tongues and crying. I wanted to participate in the grief, but hard as I tried, I couldn't fake those tears.

"Are you sad?" I turned to Tamar and whispered.

"No," she said.

"Me neither." And I wondered why.

"What do you think's gonna happen next?" I asked.

"I don't know," she said.

"Hallelujah. He's happy with Jesus now," Uncle Tim said. "He's free from his suffering. Thank the Lord. He's safe with Him." The adults kept singing and praising the Lord for taking Father David to be with Him. I could tell that the adults needed some time to grieve. We kids watched, confused. Uncle Tim pointed up to the sky that had now turned grey as the snow fell more heavily. I reluctantly sang along with their hymns of mourning.

Uncle Tim said we'd discuss details of the Family's continued existence over the next three days while reading a new book of rules issued by Mama Maria called *The Charter*. He pulled out a copy. It was about an inch thick and had a burgundy cover. There were Davidito, Father David's heir to the throne, and Mama Maria, his right-hand woman, but Father David had never issued any kind of contingency plan for after his death. He'd taught his followers to trust God and "live by faith"; he was just God's messenger.

Apparently *The Charter* would reveal instructions for the Family's future.

The adults continued with their praises and hallelujahs. Uncle Tim took out a guitar and started singing "Safe in the Arms of Jesus." I wondered why they didn't seem more shocked at the news of Father David's death. Maybe they were prepared in a way I wasn't. Soon all the adults had their eyes closed and were singing:

Safe on his gentle breast;
There by his love o'ershaded,
Sweetly my soul shall rest.

I kept my eyes open and didn't sing along. There was a part of me that felt relieved. But I had no idea of what was to come.

■ ■

WE LEARNED FROM MAMA MARIA'S newsletter that Father David had died several months earlier, but the leadership decided to keep his death under wraps until his annual birthday celebration.

He died one year after the projected date of the Great Apocalypse, in October of 1994. Had he been predicting his own demise all those years? During the four months between his death and its being revealed to the membership, some of the home shepherds and the top leadership had been made aware of the news. Mama Maria and her staff used the time to write and print *The Charter*. We also learned that the night before the big announcement, when the adults had gathered for a meeting, they received the news before the kids were told. That way they could grieve for their beloved leader, and their shock would be less apparent when it was time to tell us.

I wasn't sure how Mama Maria would continue Father David's legacy now that he was gone. In his letters she always agreed with what he said and chimed in with comments and encouragement, but her letters lacked his charisma and conviction. It was clear that she would now be first in command, and we would have to follow her rules. I wondered if the adults would submit to her with the same reverence they'd had for Father David; after all, she was a follower, like them. In her newsletter she ordered us to fast and read our new book of instructions. We were to finish it before Father David's birthday, on February 18.

After the announcement, the kids were rounded up into our regular groups. I sensed an air of unusual anticipation as the adults busily figured out what they would do next. Some of them gathered for meetings throughout the day. I'd never seen the adults so anxious. They were grieving but were also waiting to hear more news or guidance that would never come.

Over the next three days we read *The Charter* cover to cover with Auntie Esther, a young woman who was assigned to the group made up of Tamar, Mary Ann, Michelle, Sam, and me. The Family would continue to exist, *The Charter* dictated, but would now function as small, autonomous homes rather than as large, intertwined communities. The leadership would no longer have the ultimate decision regarding how we lived our lives. We could decide where and with whom we wanted to live.

The Charter outlined rules about tithing quotas and other life style choices: adults were allowed one serving of alcohol per week, either four ounces of red wine or six ounces of beer; sixteen-year-olds were allowed to have sex with eighteen-year-olds, and eighteen-year-olds were allowed to have sex with twenty-one-year-olds, but sixteen-year-olds could not have sex with twenty-one-year-olds (I was thirteen and happy I didn't have to worry about sex for a few more years). There were rules dictating what constituted a home: four consenting adults (age sixteen or older) could be considered a home and remain part of the Family, as long as they tithed 10 percent, continued to witness, and stayed updated with monthly readings of Family mailings sent out by Mama Maria and her new partner, Peter.

Auntie Esther also informed us that the Family was at the top of a list compiled by the government. The details were unclear, but the incident in Waco, Texas, involving David Koresh and his followers had made headline news in 1993. Although Father David didn't allow or promote gun ownership, he always rooted for the underdog and condemned any kind of government intrusion. He condoned Koresh's actions and beliefs in one of the last letters he wrote. Auntie Esther said after that incident the government had issued a list of "dangerous groups to watch."

"Because of our active ministry and radical beliefs, the system thinks we're dangerous," she said.

"Does that mean someone's watching us?" Mary Ann asked.

"Not watching us," Auntie Esther said. "But they are aware of our activities, so we need to be careful of our interactions with the public, especially when we're out."

"Who's going to be in charge now that Father David's dead?" Sam asked.

"Well, things are going to be different with implementation of *The Charter*," Auntie Esther said. "Individuals and families are going to have more independence and freedom, but Father David appointed Mama Maria to lead the Family, so we'll be hearing news from her."

I wondered if my family would continue living in Berwyn or if we would have to move again. Father David had formed what he called a monarchy, referring to himself as "King David" and Mama Maria as "Queen Maria." The leaders told everyone where to go and with whom to live. Living in large communities gave us a sense of support. We were poor, but we were organized, and Father David was the glue that kept the Family together. When he died, a quiet sort of anarchy ensued.

■ ■

DURING THE FAST, THE ADULTS were busy making phone calls and holding meetings. Some members had relatives who lived close by, and they opened communication with them after decades of estrangement.

On February 19, the morning after Father David's birthday celebration and three days after we'd heard the news of his death, I woke up and looked out the window. On the back lawn, everyone in the home had gathered with his or her belongings, preparing to disperse. It occurred to me that maybe the adults were happy to be granted their freedom. Perhaps this was news they had been hoping to hear for a long time. Although grieving Father David's death, they now had a choice about their living arrangements for the first time since joining the Children of God. Most of them didn't want to live in big communities, which required a great deal of work to sustain, even while providing a sense of security and support. Most had children and were probably curious to see what life would be like in a smaller living unit.

While the adults had scrambled over the previous three days to figure out where they would go next, they tried to maintain an aura of calm for the kids to shield us from knowing how different life would be going forward. Maybe they weren't aware of the changes on the horizon, or maybe they were relieved.

My family wouldn't be able to afford the house in Berwyn without a large group sharing the rent. Dad had found a small, three-bedroom house with cheap rent a few blocks away. We would live there until we found two more adults and a more permanent home. Our parents told us they still wanted to be part of the Family and to follow *The Charter*. "Our goals might be different now without Father David's guidance," Mom said, but she still seemed excited to be following his mission.

The home shepherds divided up the assets among the scattering members. As always, we didn't have much, but Uncle Tim had bought a van for the home with inheritance money he had received earlier that year. They gave our family the nine-passenger burgundy Ford van.

I took one last walk around the house. The cupboards had been cleared and the house was nearly empty. Bulky suitcases and shiny black trash bags cluttered the backyard.

"Who's gonna want to live with us?" I whispered to Tamar on the lawn.

"We're so big," she said. "And young."

I gathered for the first time that we were on our own.

CHAPTER 25

THREE MONTHS HAD PASSED SINCE we'd heard the news of Father David's death. Things had changed as we tried to maintain our membership in the Family and follow *The Charter*. We had moved into our smaller temporary home. We kept in contact with other members in the area and received monthly newsletters and mailings. We still went out to tell people about Jesus and to collect donations, but our witnessing was on a much smaller scale, as if we did it mainly for the income rather than to spread the gospel and warn people of the Apocalypse. For a while it was just our family living together, an arrangement I wasn't used to, even though I'd wished for it numerous times. We kept a daily routine that included lots of chores and minimal schooling, just the way things had been our whole lives.

We still attended services at St. Paul Thai Lutheran Church in nearby Forest Park. The white chapel was humble but beautiful, with pointed steeples, stained-glass windows, and a small cross above the front entrance. It was warm inside, and rows of wooden benches faced the pulpit next to a statue of Jesus with open arms and wearing a pastel green robe. There were fragrant flowers at the altar, announcement posters and sermons in Thai, the smiles of the Thai congregation members, and a homely kitchen in the back, where an elaborate Thai buffet was served after the sermon.

Even though Pastor Pongsak's teachings of Christ's love were much different from, and far milder, than what Father David taught, being around Thai people and Christian values at the same time felt like home. And it anchored our family.

One of the members of the Thai church was Mr. Tessalee, a Thai-Chinese man. He had three grown sons. He always wore a crisp dark suit and a skinny tie and kept his hair neatly combed. His eyes looked like slivers of the moon, and he had an infectious, wide smile. He had heard we needed a place to stay. Apparently he had money, because one day Mom announced that he owned an empty building on the South Side of Chicago, and we would be living in it rent-free.

Soon we joined with two more adults who were looking for a place to stay post-*Charter,* Uncle Steven Black and Auntie Filipino Mary, whom we had lived with in Thailand. They had three children: Daryl, Lawrence, and Bella. My brother John was fifteen and didn't count as an adult. Tamar and I were thirteen. We moved in to our new house that summer.

■ ■

IT WAS A TALL, RECTANGULAR brick building on Crystal Street near the corner of North and Pulaski in a Polish neighborhood. It had three flats that our two families would have all to ourselves, a small front yard surrounded by a rusty chain-link fence, and a small backyard that led to a garage. During the day, Puerto Ricans huddled in the alley behind the home, swapping little pieces of paper and bags and delivering hard, cold glances toward anyone who passed their way.

The upstairs kitchen was fully stocked with whatever the local warehouses could donate—miniature boxes of raisins, frozen orange juice, powdered milk, and canned beef stew. On the weekends, Dad and John sold the extra provisions that we'd collected at swap meets and flea markets. With that we had enough money for Dad to buy milk, eggs, coffee, white bread, and cereal at Omni Supermarket.

One day Dad came home and spoke to Mom in Swedish, the way they did when they had a secret to keep from us. When I asked Mom what they were talking about, she told me that Dad had started receiving money from the government. "God has many ways of providing for his children," she said. "And this is just one of them."

In Thailand I had sometimes accompanied the adults to open-air street markets, where we gathered food for free on outings we called "provisioning." When we lived in Berwyn I had been to Brickyard Mall and big-box stores like Kmart and Sam's Club to raise money by "canning" (standing outside with a sign and a collection box for food donations) and "postering" (walking around collecting donations in exchange for a colored poster of heaven). Because we got most of our food for free, I had never been to a real supermarket. Dad and Mom seemed to decide which rules they'd maintain and where they'd have to adjust or compromise. For the first time, we kids were allowed to accompany Dad when he went food shopping.

I was amazed by the abundant shelves of foods that were completely new to me: cans of corn, tomato sauce, beans, and premade soups; box after box of "fortified" cereals, some with cartoon characters grinning from the front; and so much milk and so many eggs that a whole refrigerator section was reserved for them. Besides us, the customers who crowded the store were black or

Hispanic. They wore frayed clothes that in some cases were oversized and stained. A group of teenage boys had combs stuck in their hair. They wore their pants way below their bottoms even though they had belts. They spoke English, but with an accent I had never heard.

When it came time for Dad to pay, he held his head low. He pulled out a booklet and flipped through some bills that looked like fake money. I had never seen Dad handle money before, and I wasn't sure what the fake money meant. I felt a gnawing sense of shame that began in the pit of my stomach and moved up to my throat. My face felt hot and flushed. Standing next to him made me uncomfortable. Tamar was checking out a shelf that held informational videos. Mary Ann was reading the label on the back of a cereal box.

"I don't think we belong here," I whispered to Tamar.

I had never felt shame living in Thailand, even though it was a third-world country *and* we had no money. When we lived in our large communities in Thailand and Berwyn, I didn't see people handle money, nor was I familiar with food stamps. Father David didn't recommend that we receive government assistance. Most of our food was given to us for free, and divvying up responsibilities and sharing resources with other home members in a communal setting gave us a sense of support. We didn't have a lot, but we were highly organized. Now all that was gone, and I could see that Mom and Dad were solely responsible for supporting us. Their goal was no longer following Father David and saving the world, like it had been when I was younger. I began to see that we were no longer "broke with a cause." We might actually be poor.

As I watched Dad give the grocery clerk a stack of bills, I wondered where this shame was coming from and why I had not felt it before. Had we become poor overnight? We were foreigners in our own country. Even Mr. Pongsak and his congregation seemed to notice that we were out of place.

Would I ever feel at home?

CHAPTER 26

"It's my job to keep everyone on Crystal Street safe," Mr. Roger said between glistening golden teeth. Mr. Roger lived across the street from us with the pit bull he called Butkusin in a small hatchback trailer that sat in the corner of a large junkyard. He said he was "neighborhood watch." "I stay up at nights just to make sure," he said.

It was my first real conversation with a neighbor. I stood next to Dad, observing Mr. Roger carefully. He wore a baseball cap, from which his hair coiled out underneath. His grimy skin was almost black. The creases on his neck resembled a map of the Amazon River. All his top front teeth were missing, and little metal caps were revealed when he smiled wide. He had a wooden peg for a leg and spoke with a Southern drawl. I had never seen anyone so grungy. He looked like one of Father David's lonely bums in his evangelical comic books—someone who was lost and needed to be saved.

One day Mom decided that Mr. Roger needed to know God's message, so she invited him over for dinner. "Never pass up an opportunity to tell someone about Jesus," she said. We sat around the table eating fish sticks with ketchup and steamed rice while Mom told him about Jesus. Outside, the sweltering heat was subsiding into fall. When I looked at his neck I could tell that he must have had the equivalent of a shower for this occasion because the grime on his neck was less visible.

We continued to try to keep the daily routine that we'd followed in the Family. Mom divided up the chores. There were now eleven kids in our family, plus Steven and Mary's three children. Mom put me in charge of taking care of toddlers Brian, Suzy, and Bella. Tamar cooked lunch and dinner every day and cleaned the kitchen, dining room, and living room. Mary Ann's job was to take care of Mikey and Lawrence, whom we called Loey Toey. Mom, who was pregnant with her twelfth child, took care of Becky and Daryl, both seven. Heidi was in charge of Bobby, who was one. Dad, John, and Uncle Steven were responsible for getting the money we needed for food and utilities. Since we didn't have to pay rent, we didn't have to worry about that expense.

We joined the Riverside Public Library. I'd grown up with only two kinds of reading material: the Bible, and the missives and books of Father David. We knew other books existed, but we never read or even saw them. In America that changed for us. Now during naptime I read books I had borrowed from the library. The Little House on the Prairie series was my favorite. I loved the way Laura Ingalls Wilder described the details of her wholesome childhood. After reading at night I rocked Brian to sleep and sang songs to him that I remembered from the Family. I devised a daytime schedule of school and play to keep the toddlers busy. One day Mom told me it was time for Brian to learn to read. She handed me a giant book called *Teach Your Child to Read in 100 Easy Lessons*. It was about an inch thick with wide pages full of lessons and exercises. Three months later, at two-and-a-half years old, Brian could read fluently.

We continued attending the Thai church. They included us in their after-church activities; invited us on a retreat and to family parties; taught us traditional Thai dance; and asked Tamar, Mary Ann, Heidi, and me to be flower girls and candle lighters for weddings and performances.

Mom and Dad never talked about leaving the Family, and neither did my siblings and I. But I could tell from the look of exhaustion on their faces from the routine of taking care of our family that serving God and following Father David's teachings were no longer their priorities; their primary concern was feeding our family and finding ways to make ends meet.

■ ■

WHEN WINTER CAME, LAKE MICHIGAN froze into a solid block of ice. We stored the milk on the stairwell to keep it cold. Sometimes we woke up to gallons of slushy or frozen milk. Snow pelted down in torrents and, once settled on the ground, turned into brown, muddy slush. The wind had a character all its own. It whispered in the spring, hibernated in the summer, and kicked into a frenzied mood in fall. By winter the wind seemed to have the authority to lower the temperature at will. Zero degrees could feel like negative fifty depending on how fast the wind blew off the Great Lakes. I liked the idea of the wind chill factor. It made the weather mathematical, like an equation: you could multiply the temperature outside by the mood of the wind and come up with a whole new result. It was flexible and malleable, not static like the hardened ice on the surface of Lake Michigan.

Tamar, Mary Ann, Heidi, and I, along with a few other members who lived nearby, formed a singing group to raise money. We learned Christmas songs in Spanish, perfecting our accents, and sang them for customers at various Mexican restaurants on Pulaski Street in the Hispanic district. People listened while eating their enchiladas dripping with cheese sauce, crispy tacos, and colossal burritos oozing with meat, lettuce, and tomatoes. We wore matching frilly dresses, stockings decorated with holly designs, and tinsel halos. After our performance, the restaurant exploded into a roar of applause. We walked from table to table selling cassette tapes, produced in Japan, that featured the Family's renditions of traditional Christmas carols like "O Holy Night" and "Little Drummer Boy." We closed with "Feliz Navidad." Our feet were exhausted from treading the cold, slushy sidewalks. Our bones shivered from wearing only frilly dresses and tights. The owner of the last restaurant where we performed fed us a feast of Mexican delicacies. I had never tasted so much delicious food on one plate at the same time.

■ ■

As a family, the one thing we owned was the nine-passenger van with comfortable red velvet bench seats that Uncle Tim had given to us when we left the Berwyn house. One day John looked out the window and noticed that it was gone. Stolen. We saw it later, when the thieves drove by in it. They slowed down as they passed our building, as if to say, "Come get us!" Some days later we found our van parked a few blocks away. The windows were smashed, the carpet torn out, the doors ripped from their hinges.

The spare tire was missing. It had been stripped of its wheels, seats, stereo, steering wheel, and engine. All that was left was the metal body, sitting there like a sturdy tent.

Now we had nothing. At Dad's request, Roger hired a towing company to take the shell of the van to Roger's junkyard. For a while afterward, I could see the van shining above the pile of metal that cluttered the yard. It was the same deep, gleaming red it had always been. It reminded me of our family: it wasn't even proper scrap for a junkyard. Our family didn't belong in that neighborhood. The thought never occurred to me, however, that we needed to get out.

■ ■

BUT MAYBE MOM AND DAD were thinking about moving. Auntie Mary, Dad's older sister, with whom we had lived in Eagle Rock, had settled in La Habra, California, with her husband, Uncle Nick from New York, and their six children. Before that, they had spent several years at the HCS in Japan. We had heard that her two older boys, Robert and Ivan, had left the Family and were now systemites. They had been, as she put it, "real troublemakers" in Japan and were often assigned to "Victor Programs." Father David labeled anyone who rebelled against the Children of God "bad apples," capable of spoiling the whole barrel if they weren't put swiftly into check. Victor Programs were implemented as ways to isolate the "bad apples" before their doubts about the Family spread to the younger kids. The teens quarantined in Victor Programs were separated from the rest of the home, kept under a watchful eye, and made to memorize scripture. They were subject to humiliating disciplinary actions if they disobeyed or protested, and they were held to a strict schedule from the time they rose until nighttime, when they crashed into bed from exhaustion.

In the photos Auntie Mary sent us, Robert and Ivan wore sunglasses and had long hair. I could tell they had been contaminated by the system, but as much as I thought I should judge them and label them "backsliders," they instead intrigued me. What was this world like? And why was it forbidden?

Auntie Mary also sent pictures of her house in California. It was surrounded by bougainvillea and had English ivy crawling up the brick walls. She told us in a letter that she had talked the landlord into a reduced-rent agreement. With her soothing phone voice, she had a gift for getting things for free. She was often part of her home's provisioning team.

John flew out to California to visit Auntie Mary, who had found him a cheap deal on an airline ticket. When he returned home, his hair was slicked back and he wore store-bought clothes. He looked like the systemites in Father David's comic books. He sometimes wore headphones. He must have been listening to system music. He'd always been obsessed with his outward appearance and with building muscles. Was he becoming a systemite, I wondered?

John brought good news. Aunt Mary had found a place for us to live near her family in the San Gabriel Valley. The Chicago winters were too cold, and California offered perfect weather, endless summers, and rain that fell in sprinkles.

I remembered living in campgrounds along California's coastlines when I was four. I recalled staying in the house next to my grandpa's. There was a large peach tree in the front yard and two avocado varieties in the back. Every summer the peaches ripened into ornaments the color of Saturn. We rubbed their fuzz across our cheeks and examined the minute hairs. I didn't care much about eating the peaches; I was just fascinated with the fuzz. And I knew that the Children of God had started on the shores of California, in Huntington Beach.

Father David had talked a lot about how California, his birth state, was doomed and would be the first place to "sink into the sea" after an earthquake or some other sign of the End Time. Otherwise, I didn't know much about Dad's original home, the "Golden State." Mom said it would take four days to drive to California, if we kept potty breaks to a minimum and only stopped to eat and sleep. We had a new van by then. Dad and John, selling the surplus groceries we'd obtained for free, had saved enough money to buy a Dodge that Mom had found in the *PennySaver*. The ad stated that it was "not safe to be used for children," but she said we didn't have much of a choice. "We can't always decide how God will provide for his children." The van was off-white and longer than the other, with patches of rust and an exhaust pipe that spouted curly puffs of black smoke whenever Dad started it.

Uncle Steven Black and Auntie Filipino Mary weren't coming with us. They had found relatives to stay with in Texas, Uncle Steven's home state.

■ ■

ON THE MORNING OF OUR departure we ate a hearty breakfast of scrambled eggs and white-bread toast. Then we piled into the van. It was the beginning of April and the end of a long, cold winter. Dad had hitched a wooden wagon to the back and loaded it with foam mattresses and our meager luggage. Dad and John would take turns driving. Tamar had made tuna salad sandwiches for the trip. The older kids took turns holding baby Bobby because we didn't have a child car seat. Mom lay sprawled across the front bench seat, just behind the driver's seat, her stomach bulging with child number twelve. She seemed tired frequently in those days, and I could tell it wasn't just because she was pregnant; something seemed wrong. She preferred lying down instead of sitting and often complained of pains in her stomach.

Just before we pulled out of the alley, a boy showed up at the side of our van. He had a shaved head, like most of the Puerto Ricans who lived on our block. Mom pressed down the lock on her door and told anyone who was near a door to do the same. The boy wore an oversized T-shirt partly tucked in, exposing a wedge of belt. The hems of his baggy pants bunched over his tennis shoes. He had a tattoo behind his left ear. We kept quiet as he approached. He circled the van once and then pulled something out of his belt. I could see that it was a gun. He slid his finger into the trigger and gave us a cold, hard look, tilting his head in a demonstration of superiority and pride. I felt myself shrink. The boy swung the gun around a few times. I imagined what he was thinking: *You watch your backs, gringos. You leave now, and don't you dare come back.* Then he turned around and walked away, his shoulders broader and his chest higher. Mom told Dad we should probably leave. Dad put the key in the ignition and started the engine. It reluctantly revved to life.

"California, here we come," Mom said.

"California, here we come!" we kids responded in unison.

CHAPTER 27

As THE SUN DISAPPEARED BEHIND a landscape of low-lying mountains and purple clouds, a song from Kenny Loggins came on the radio. Dad sang along in the same voice he used to sing to us at the campgrounds in California:

And even though we ain't got money,
I'm so in love with you, honey.

He glanced back at Mom.
"This is my song to you, babes," he said.
"Yeah, honey," she said. "Especially the 'we ain't got money' part."

We pulled into a driveway close to midnight. The air was crisp and the sky clear, with a few stars sprinkled throughout. Auntie Mary had arranged for us to live temporarily in the town of Placentia, in North Orange County, until a larger house in nearby Diamond Bar was ready for us. The home in Diamond Bar was reportedly so big that each of us might only have to share a room with one other person. I was thrilled at the thought of having my "almost own" room.

In our temporary house, off Limerick Drive, mattresses were sprawled across the floor of the living room. It was warm when we arrived except for a somber breeze. The living room had a lofty ceiling, and a couple of fans spun. We pretended we were having a slumber party, like we used to in the compounds on dress-up night, and fell asleep on the mattresses.

The next morning, we set up the TV on the coffee table right away, found the signal, and tuned in to the local channels, which broadcast national news, sitcoms, and chatty talk shows. We quickly also discovered MTV and the E! channel, with their features on colorful pop stars and glamorous supermodels and celebrities. I had entertainment to last me for days.

From our house, whichever way you walked, you could find a shopping center and a supermarket or parks with lakes and rolling hills. I could tell it was a much safer neighborhood than the one surrounding our house on Crystal Street in Chicago. We took a family outing to Tri-City Park for a picnic. It was a perfect day with radiant skies. The clear blue lake, where geese and ducks swam and waddled along the banks, was lined with eucalyptus trees. The sun shone high, and the streets leading to the park were lined with palm trees. Ficus trees were abundant, and bougainvillea sprawled along brick walls.

We met our cousins Ivan and Robert at the park. They wore sporty sunglasses and oversized clothes with light athletic jackets that read "Adidas" even though it wasn't cold. I could tell by their choice of attire, slouched posture, and "cool" demeanor that they had clearly become systemites. Although I had read and heard about systemites and about backsliding teens and YAs, I had never seen one up close, and I never would have imagined someone from my own family becoming one. Could I also become a systemite? Was California going to change me too, like it had changed them?

■ ■

THREE MONTHS LATER WE MOVED to Diamond Bar. Now that the Family was starting to fall apart, most of the members who had resided in this house had moved on, either to live with or near relatives who could help them out, or to explore other cities or countries.

Compared to the house on Crystal Street, our new home seemed like a mansion. We called it Windows. It looked nothing like the typical houses in the neighborhood, which seemed to mostly resemble each other with their perfectly manicured yards. Windows was asymmetrical and awkward, built on unstable ground at the top of a steep hill. The angles were uneven, as if the architect had changed his mind midway during construction. The ceiling sloped downward, and the paint color varied, in some places seemingly midway through a brushstroke. The entrance was located on the side of the house instead of in the front. At the bottom of the driveway a wooden placard read, in fancy letters, "5429." We were home—at least for the time being.

The house's spacious interior had sliding glass doors in almost every room. On a clear day, I could see the Hollywood sign from the living room, even though it was thirty miles away. At night, the valley lit up into a flickering sea of dazzling sparkles. On hot summer evenings, a cool breeze freshened the place, a reminder that Southern California is really a Mediterranean-like oasis stuck in the middle of a desert. But on most days a thick blanket of smog settled in the valley, allowing for the most magnificent sunsets at night.

The owner of the house had never seen it. It had been given to him as collateral by someone who owed him a debt that they couldn't pay off. We paid $1,900 a month in rent, even though it was on a million-dollar lot and surrounded by multimillion-dollar mansions. Auntie Mary had talked the owner into accepting reduced rent by telling him that we'd done charity work overseas. She had pictures of us at orphanages helping with hunger relief after a flood.

John got his first job tearing tickets at Edwards Cinema, a low-budget movie theater in Brea to which he rode his bike every day. He always worked hard; Mom told stories of his making breakfast on his own when he was four years old. He soon found a second job at a bagel shop. I had never known someone with a real job and an actual boss and a paycheck, and I secretly admired his ambition. He left the house in the mornings wearing a blue-collared shirt buttoned all the way except for the top button. He came home late at night smelling of coffee, his hands stained black from handling the grounds. He saved enough money for his first car, a midnight-blue 1963 Volkswagen bug. When he brought it home we kids climbed in and explored it, inhaling the smell of leather as we pretended to shift gears.

That July, Mom was induced. She had Vinny in a hospital in Placentia. We took turns holding him and snapping pictures, like we always did when Mom brought home a newborn. Vinny was child number twelve, bringing the total to six boys and six girls, age sixteen and under. After Vinny's birth, Mom started making frequent trips to the hospital. She had an "abnormality" the doctors wanted to investigate.

CHAPTER 28

THE FAMILY LEADERS MUST HAVE grown concerned at the dropout rates following Father David's death, especially among the younger generation after the famous walkout in Europe. In an attempt to convince the younger teens that the Family was "cool," the few remaining leaders in Southern California arranged for a group of us to take a camping trip to Lake Tahoe. Uncle Tim, whom we had lived with in Chicago and who had also moved to Southern California, was the team captain. He drove a big blue bus adorned with cartoon pictures and colorful graffiti.

Since moving to the house on Crystal Street, we hadn't been under constant adult supervision. In Thailand, Mary Ann was often labeled a "problem child," like Robert and Ivan were in

Japan, and put on special programs or quarantined. Now, even though Uncle Tim was hardly authoritarian, being under the watchful eye of an adult again made something in Mary Ann snap.

"This isn't right," she said one afternoon while we sat on a campground picnic bench, eating blueberry pie filling from a large can, one of the food items we had provisioned for our road trip. "We don't want to be part of this anymore."

Tamar and I agreed. We'd had doubts and questions about the Family for a while.

"What should we do about it?" I asked.

"Let's call home and tell Mom," Mary Ann said.

"Tell Mom what?" Tamar asked.

"That we want a *normal* high school experience. We want a *normal* life," Mary Ann said.

At that picnic table, surrounded by towering pines, Mary Ann, Tamar, and I decided we wanted nothing more to do with the Family. We were finished. We wanted out. We found a campground pay phone, and Mary Ann dialed home. In the distance the view of Lake Tahoe on the horizon cut through the forest. The sky was clear and blue with a few puffs of white clouds. Mom answered.

"We don't want to be part of this anymore," Mary Ann said. "We're done!"

"We want to go to school," Tamar and I chimed in. "We want to experience high school and have friends. We want to be normal."

"Okay. That's fine. Your brother left too," Mom said, referring to John, who'd begun staying out late and bringing home strange friends who chain-smoked cigarettes and went to all-night parties called "raves." She sounded defeated. We knew that John had been partying and hanging out with our cousins Ivan and Robert, but the revelation that he had moved out came as a shock, although I was also secretly intrigued by the prospect of leaving the Family. The world outside was a forbidden temptation and I had thought of it countless times as a child, but never imagined that it was actually possible. With John leaving, the prospect was now within reach. I didn't want to disappoint my parents, but I wondered, along with Tamar and Mary Ann, would we be next?

"We just want what's best for you," Mom continued, "and if that's what you want, then that's fine. Your dad can enroll you in high school as soon as you get back."

We hadn't expected her to agree so readily, especially after hearing about other parents who'd sent their kids out into the world alone, without support.

Mom said she had news for us too. The three of us strained to hear her over the receiver.

"I got the results back from the doctor today," she said. "The results were positive. I have cancer."

We fell silent. Maybe that's why she hadn't resisted our demand. With her health now a priority, maybe her dedication to the Family and its mission of saving the world had faded.

"What does that mean?" Mary Ann asked. We had heard the word *cancer*. We knew it was deadly, and we knew it may have been what killed Father David (although we were never sure), but we never knew anyone who had been diagnosed until now.

"It's cervical cancer," Mom said.

She told us that she would have surgery soon to see if they could remove the tumors from her uterus. If not, she'd have to have radiation. Chemo would be a last resort.

When we got home we weren't aware of the seriousness of Mom's situation, only that things were going to be different; she wouldn't be able to have any more babies, and she'd have to start seeing the doctor on a regular basis.

Later, Mom told me that when she was pregnant with Tamar and me, the doctor had told her something was "abnormal."

"We didn't think anything of it," she said. "Since the world was going to end anyway."

CHAPTER 29

A FEW WEEKS AFTER OUR trip to Lake Tahoe, Dad enrolled Tamar, Mary Ann, and me in a home-schooling supplemental course called HOPES: Home Opportunity Program for Educational Success. It was located in a portable building off Walnut Drive. Across the street stood a video store with the letters *XXX* blaring in neon on the window. We met once a week to turn in last week's homework and receive new assignments. The principal of HOPES, Mr. Utsler, had a mouth that shifted to one side when he talked and bloodshot eyes that were hidden behind thick glasses. His belly protruded over his pants.

I was fifteen years old and had never attended a real school. This was my first step toward a normal, future, and I was thrilled.

Even though Mom was receiving weekly radiation treatments, she still cheered us on in our decision to go to school.

Some of the kids at HOPES were older and were there to obtain their high school diplomas. Some were single mothers who didn't have time to attend school full-time. We were there because, Dad said, "Putting you girls in public school would be like dumping a couple of lambs into a lion's den." He was probably right.

I had never spoken to kids outside the Family, and I saw my first opportunity with a girl named Kristen. From making observations at the mall and elsewhere, I had learned to determine a person's "coolness" by the clothes they wore. This was the nineties. Cool boys wore loose clothes—usually a button-down checkered shirt worn open over a white undershirt or a tank top—and skater or tennis shoes. They carried their skateboards and walked with other cool boys and usually one or two cool girls. Girls had more clothing options because they could wear dresses and skirts, but in general girls looked the coolest when they mimicked the boys' apparel as closely as possible without looking like a boy. They sported baggy cargo pants with dangling silver key chains and soft white cotton tank tops. Androgynous jewelry and neutral-colored backpacks were also cool. Jeans were acceptable for both genders, and for girls, dyed hair and heavy makeup. Music (the right kind), drugs, and the occasional cigarette were cool.

Kristen fit the bill for "cool." She wore deep-colored flannel shirts, jeans, heavy jewelry, and thick makeup that accentuated her eyebrows and lip line. We didn't have time to socialize at HOPES since we were there so infrequently, so I decided to start my first conversation with a systemite and hopefully make my first friend by writing Kristen a friendly note.

Dear Kristen,

I would like to be your friend. Maybe we could hang out outside of school. Here is my number: (909) 555-3485. Feel free to call me anytime.

Flor

I slipped her the folded note one day when school was almost out. She opened it, read it, looked at me, and never spoke to me or looked my way again.

■ ■

AFTER A YEAR AT HOPES, thanks to Mary Ann's campaigning backed up by Tamar and me, we registered at Rowland High School. I got kicked out on my first day for showing too much cleavage. Mrs. Buck, my second-period Spanish teacher, invited me to return to school wearing appropriate clothing. I'd never been taught to be ashamed of my body. After that incident I wore turtlenecks to school.

Rowland High was full of cool boys and girls. Groups of skaters and kids on low-rider bikes congregated on street corners with their baggy pants hanging low on their bums, smoking weed and cigarettes, stalling before going to class. Kids who looked like they had stepped out of an eighties punk-rock movie paraded through campus dressed in tattered black Pantera or Grateful Dead T-shirts. They wore their hair in multicolored Mohawks and used safety pins to close the holes in their clothes. Veronica, a thickset girl who dressed in jeans and purple T-shirts, hung out with the punk kids. She made it a point to sputter, "Gutter twins!" every day when she passed us.

"Why does she call us gutter twins?" I asked Tamar.

"I have no idea."

"Maybe because we're not from around here?"

"Yup, that could be it," she said. "We're aliens."

Tamar and I noticed a Thai girl named Diana. We let her know right away that we had grown up in Thailand. It was the only common ground we had. Diana wore pastel checkered shirts and plain dark jeans that had no shape or style. Her hair was always tied back in a loose ponytail, and she never wore makeup. Her voice was low in pitch, and unlike the other girls we encountered at high school, she listened when we talked.

"So, why'd you guys grow up in Thailand?" Diana asked us one day when we met up for lunch.

"Our dad was an English teacher," Tamar said triumphantly, like she actually meant it. I was starting to let Tamar speak for me. We hadn't had a conversation to decide what we would say if someone asked us about our past.

"So, what does your dad do for a living?" Diana asked.

Tamar looked at me. We both looked down at the concrete. There was an awkward silence, then a gurgle from Tamar's throat.

"Well, our dad was an English teacher in Thailand," she said. Sometimes we told people he was in the military. Both were half-truths since some of the adults did take up English-teaching jobs at military base camps to obtain visas and make some extra cash.

"Yeah, but what does he do *now?*" Diana persisted.

Tamar's face turned red. I felt my cheeks flush. I decided to keep quiet.

"Um, I don't know. . . . I mean, he does. . . stuff," Tamar said. "Uh, he teaches."

"Where does he teach?"

"Um, I don't know," Tamar said. "I'll have to ask him."

Diana gave us a long, hard look. She never met us for lunch after that.

■ ■

TO PASS TIME AFTER CLASS, I walked to the public library on Nogales Street. Our lives were very different now from how they'd been before. We watched TV, including soap operas, and read books and magazines. I was drawn to the magazine section in the library. I gazed at the celebrities and supermodels on the covers. I read articles and interviews with movie stars I had never heard of. Based on the photos I looked at, they seemed happy. And they were rich. I became obsessed with how they made becoming rich and living with fame look so easy, so natural. I became convinced that within myself was the same potential to be just as good-looking, just as rich, and maybe even famous. The pictures told me that good looks, riches, and fame equaled happiness beyond my wildest dreams. I sucked it all up. My brain was like a sponge, searching for any truth to absorb.

In February, the Oscars aired, and Tamar and I moved the TV to our room for the afternoon. During the five-hour broadcast, including the arrivals special, we ate air-popped popcorn and gawked at the celebrities parading down the red carpet in their ball gowns and sharp tuxedos. We were completely beside ourselves with awe. So rich. So talented. So beautiful! How were we excluded from this elaborate procession?

One day I picked up an issue of *Seventeen* magazine. On the front cover a girl smiled, flaunting perfectly aligned, pearly-white teeth. Her straight blond hair hung over her delicate shoulders. She wore a red halter top and had tiny freckles sprinkled across the bridge of her nose and her cheekbones. I flipped through the pages. In a sidebar, my eyes fell on a question posed in bold black letters: "Did You Grow Up in a Cult: Take This Quiz and Find Out Now."

The words slashed through my mind, piercing through my doubts. I turned the pages. The questions seemed to glare at me:

"Did you grow up in a secluded environment?" I thought about the homes with high walls. Yes.

"Were you under the influence of a charismatic leader?" I thought about Father David and all the leaders. Yes!

"Were you coerced to recruit members to your group?" I thought about how we went witnessing to recruit souls for God's Heavenly Kingdom. Absolutely.

"Were you prohibited from leaving the premises unless you were recruiting members?" Uh-huh.

"Were you taught that the world outside was a forbidden place, and did you feel guilty for wanting to leave?" Bingo!

"If you have answered yes to at least three of the last five questions, then you may have grown up in a cult." I had answered yes to all five.

My eyes opened. For a moment my world shifted out of orbit. There was a clear reason why I felt like an outsider. My heart was racing, my throat parched. Everything around me was spinning. I snuck the magazine out of the library and showed Tamar and Mary Ann the quiz.

"You're not gonna believe this," I said, barely able to get the words out. "We grew up in a cult."

But for Mary Ann it was old news. Even though she didn't use the word *cult,* she had known something was up for a while.

"That's obvious," Mary Ann said bluntly. "There's nothing we can do about it. The leaders are at fault, and they get away with it. They're the tyrants. We're the victims. Now we have to pay the price." She sounded defeated, but I could tell she was also hurt and angered by the way she had been treated in the Family—being put in isolation and served humiliating punishments for questioning the teachings of Father David.

I thought about the "homes" we'd lived in. They were really compounds. Father David was a Koresh-like leader who kept us isolated from the world as he conjured a utopian afterlife to look forward to—a utopia that would never come. Now I was thrust into the present.

"Do you understand what this means?" I said, stumbling over my words. "This wasn't our choice. We were lied to our whole lives."

I could barely speak. An avalanche of thoughts overwhelmed me as I began to unravel the knots of my past. I never chose to join the Children of God, but I had been forced to stay, like all the other second-generation children. I was never given the option to leave or to make my own decisions. I started to see my parents in a new light. They were no longer innocent. I was a victim. But they were also victims, both of Father David and of the mainstream world they were trying to escape in joining the Children of God. Who could I blame? Father David was dead. My parents were struggling to make it in the world; as hard as I tried, I couldn't be mad at them. I felt myself turn bitter and cold. I kept repeating those few words over and over.

"Oh my God! I grew up in a cult. OH MY GOD! I grew up in a cult!"

For the next few days I walked around in a blur and in shock. I felt violated. I had been cheated. My childhood had been stolen from me. Where was I to turn? As I grappled to make sense of the past, only one thing was clear: I now had the language to define what I had been through: *cult.* What did it mean? I found myself sinking deeper and deeper into questions and confusion. My world had come undone but somehow made perfect sense at the same time. How was I going to cope? How I had grown up was not normal. Everything I had been taught as a child was a lie:

from the Apocalypse to the return of Jesus to how I was special and chosen by God.

This life-changing news didn't hit me all at once. Layers of reaction unfolded over time—days, months, years. I knew there was no way to go back and change things in the past, but I was here, alive, and for now all I could do was cope with the present—the unbearable now.

My siblings and I reacted to this newfound truth about our childhoods in different ways. John held down multiple jobs and after work stayed out all night with his friends, partying in the rave scene. Mary Ann had frequent breakdowns and started acting strange, dressing in colorful clothes and telling her friends to "eat dirt" (for a while that was all she said to anyone). Heidi spent much of her time away from home with new friends who lived down the street and dressed in black, wore smeared eye makeup, and chain-smoked cigarettes. She started listening to bands like Nirvana and Rage Against the Machine. One day she came home with a neat row of razor slits on the insides of her wrists. When Dad drilled her about it, she said, "Shut up. How dare you tell me what to do? You raised us in a cult!" Soon this was our response to our parents' every attempt to manage us.

My appearance became my rebellion. I cut my hair and dyed it an awful carrot color. I complemented my new hairstyle by wearing jeans, jewelry, tennis shoes—anything that had been forbidden. Because the now was too difficult to cope with, Tamar and I took to drinking alcohol, smoking pot, and hanging out with friends who took drugs we had never heard of. Stores, those mysterious treasure houses filled with an alluring array of goods, were too tempting. The four of us older girls began shoplifting regularly. School became our haven from the confusing realities of home, and every day after school Tamar and I made it a point to stay out for as long as we could.

CHAPTER 30

As PART OF OUR REBELLION Tamar and I tried to fit in at school. We made a cool-seeming friend named Claudia. All her friends called her Crayola because she dressed colorfully and carried a metal lunch box that looked like a box full of crayons. It dangled from her small, bony wrist like it was a permanent decorative extension. Her knuckles were clunky with skull-and-bones rings, and she wore lots of thick chain jewelry.

Crayola's bangs were dyed pink, and she wore bright red or hot-pink lipstick and fake eyelashes that were sometimes streaked with blue or purple. She had a bright smile and was easy to find at lunch break or after class because her colorful clothes were adorned with stripes or polka dots or rainbows—or a combination of all three. She wore Doc Martens lace-up steel-toe boots with fishnet stockings that made her skinny legs look like sticks. Sometimes she wore an overcoat of fake fur even though it wasn't cold outside.

Crayola lived in a house on Nausika Avenue with a blue paint job that made it stand out from the houses surrounding it. We passed it every day on our way home from school. From the outside it looked like an ordinary house, but Crayola told us that it was a residential home for girls.

"I have to follow strict rules to stay there," she said. She had to be home by a certain time every day, but she often violated her curfew. She had to check in if she wanted to go out beyond school hours. She wasn't allowed to drink or do drugs, and she wasn't allowed to have guests over. We never asked her why she lived there, but we knew it had something to do with her parents not being able to handle her anymore. She told us they had kicked her out of her house many times because of her wild behavior. Maybe that's why we liked her. She didn't have a real home and neither did we. She was an outcast and so were we. We learned to care for outsiders like us. They were our new family. Crayola told us that we were her new best friends, and we were thrilled.

Crayola was a wild thing. She once pulled me into a Taco Bell bathroom near campus and asked me in a drunken slur if I had ever kissed a girl. I told her that I hadn't, and she pulled me close and kissed me hard on the lips. I had to wipe off the smear of pink lipstick from around my mouth before exiting the bathroom.

Crayola loved to drink, and she carried some form of hard liquor with her at all times. Between class periods she would pull us into the girls' restroom and retrieve a bottle of Jack Daniel's or peppermint schnapps or cheap vodka from her bright pink or purple Jansport backpack. We'd take turns nursing the bottle until the blue tiles around us started to spin. After downing nearly the whole bottle, we stumbled our way back to class. Somehow we managed to maintain straight As, despite the spinning.

I started coming home from school drunk. I would shout at Mom and Dad, "You raised us in a cult! How could you? I hate you! How dare you! I should've never been born! You should've never had any of us!"

John still worked a lot and spent most nights partying with his friends. After a brief stint in high school, Mary Ann decided to get her GED, but she had begun to grow distant from Tamar and me.

I couldn't acknowledge where I had come from or accept the fact that this moment was all there was. Growing up, I had been told that I was chosen. I had lived for the promise of the End Time, but now there was no end in sight—no utopia, no heaven to look forward to. As a preteen, I had thought America held the promise of "cool" and glamour, of acceptance and happiness. But now, that too seemed to be slipping away. To cope with the this new "normal" that I so desperately wanted to escape, I'd get as drunk as I possibly could and turn my mind into a spinning cycle of forgetfulness, a carefree void.

I also developed a deep reverence for anyone with a tendency to cause a ruckus. The outcasts were my allies. Anyone who had a rebellious streak was my friend. And I had no boundaries when it came to obeying the orders of my new comrades. They drank heavily and wanted me to as well, so I did. Besides blunting my confusion, getting drunk gave me a sense of dignity because I was fitting in.

I started to play a game with myself in which I attempted to see how much I could drink and still maintain my sanity. Even when the world around me started to spin and I slipped in and out of blackness, there was a center inside of me that said, "Don't lose it. You got this. Don't let anyone know how far you've gone." I hid my belligerence. I masked my intoxication. I developed a sense of self-control, and it was my newfound identity. It made me feel proud. It made me feel invincible. Since I had control over nothing else in my life, at least I could control my wild drinking.

My drinking became a source of entertainment for both myself and those around me. When our new friends said to Tamar and me, "Pound liquor," we did it. When they said, "Down a forty in one shot," we did that. And when they said, "Steal a bottle at Thrifty's. We'll watch for security. You won't get caught. I promise," we did that too. Tamar and I found acceptance in humiliating ourselves according to their wishes.

I didn't care about living anymore, but the less I cared, the more invincible I felt. Once, after following my friends' orders to steal a bottle of vodka, I ran across the street, flipped over the hood of a white Honda Accord while it was moving, then got up, vodka in tow, and barely missed getting struck by a semi while my friends stood at the stoplight and watched.

Drunken rages at Rowland Heights Park, located down the street from our high school, became an after-school routine. One day we were there with Crayola and Thomas—her boyfriend, who was older and hadn't graduated because he had been expelled for being drunk on campus—and their circle of friends. These kids skated in places they weren't supposed to skate and tagged graffiti on the sides of freeway overpasses. Thomas retrieved a bottle of vodka from his backpack. We drank it straight. It felt like fire down my throat and made my ears burn. We drank it like it was medicine that would erase our childhood wounds with each desperate sip. We were walking away from the park when Thomas, drunk as usual, mentioned that he would have kissed me if he weren't with Crayola. Hearing this, Crayola approached me from behind and hit me on the head with her lunch box. I fell to the ground, partly from the vodka, and she started yanking my hair by its roots, shouting, "You fucking bitch!"

Since she was much smaller than me, I pulled myself out of her grasp. Tamar and I walked home together, crying, to the sound of Crayola still yelling.

Everything was spinning when I got home. I felt like a failure. The only person besides Tamar who I thought was my friend had just rejected me. How was I ever going to survive in this world? How was I going to fit in? Triggered by the fight with Crayola and distraught over my falling-apart family, I recalled the stories of other kids who couldn't cope after leaving the Family and attempted to take their own lives. I decided to look for a way to end it all.

I searched the house for anything that could cause death by ingestion—bleach, pills, a combination of cleaning products. I wanted it to be quick and painless, but I didn't want to mangle my body. I found a nearly full bottle of aspirin in Mom's cupboard. I decided that, on top of all the vodka I had drunk, it would do the trick nicely. I grabbed a piece of paper and a pen and headed off to my favorite hideout, tucked on a hill behind a farmhouse. There, before taking the pills, I found a sort of peace.

I had grown up in a world where I was prohibited from making decisions. But if there's one freedom we have as humans, it's the will to live or die. I recalled a scene from the 1993 version of *The Three Musketeers,* one of the first movies we watched after moving to the U.S. Milady de Winter is sentenced to beheading for treason. Moments before her execution, clad in a flowing white gown, she jumps off a rocky cliff to her death in the ocean below.

There's a euphoria that accompanies the ultimate choice. There are color and light. There's acceptance. People who want to die are not, in that moment, depressed. They are very much alive—maybe too alive. Their physical senses are heightened. There is so much beauty in, say, the color of a traffic light, the sound of a lawnmower in the early afternoon, or a song that comes on the radio at the perfect time. Such beauty fills you with equal parts dread and euphoria so that there is no difference between the two. It's pure feeling. Pure sound, energy, light, vibration. There is no judgment. That's what wanting to die feels like. It's indefinable. It's beautiful. Some even say it's art.

In the Family, we never talked about suicide, but the "End" was always on the horizon. When you've lived a life where death is an arm's reach away, the prospect is enticing *and* feasible. Because I had thought of heaven so much as a child, I'd always felt connected to the afterlife in a way most people weren't, almost like I belonged *there* instead of *here*. It wasn't a way out; it was a way in. Life—even in all its magic and beauty—is a slow journey to death, so why not end it now? Why not meet the "light"?

■ ■

BEFORE HEADING TO THE HILL, I had written Mom and Dad a suicide note. It said I was unable to handle the world. I was sorry and I loved them and would miss them. And I loved and would miss Tamar. I would miss her the most. But I didn't want them to miss me. I would be fine. And Tamar would be fine. Death is just a journey and one that I'd prepared for my whole life.

I swallowed the pills in handfuls until the bottle was almost empty. I took the last pills one by one.

Once the sun had set I stumbled to my room and went to bed expecting, like I did most nights as a child, that I wouldn't wake up. I prayed I would die in my sleep, painlessly, my body still intact.

CHAPTER 31

I WAS AWAKE ALL NIGHT, throwing up a poisonous combination of vodka and remnants of over-the-counter painkillers. Every time I looked at myself in the mirror, I couldn't bear what I saw. How could I live with myself?

Tamar came into the bathroom, and I told her what I had done. She hugged me and said she sometimes thought about ending her life too, but remember how she had tried to go to heaven when she was a little girl and it didn't work?

Like a cat, I seemed to have multiple lives: I had almost died while being born, my foot dangling out of Mom's body for nineteen minutes; I'd been hit by a car earlier that year; the machete incident with Dad and Uncle Paul; and now this. I had been given a free pass. After surviving the suicide attempt, I made a promise to myself that I would never try to end my life again.

I mustered up my best outfit, walked onto the school campus, and held my head high. As I headed to first-period science class, I resolved I was going to have to keep looking up. I was going to have to find a way—*any way*—to keep hope alive. Because if death doesn't accept you when you knock at its door, I sure as hell didn't know what would.

In class my stomach ached from the overdose of pills and my throat burned from the rancid taste of bile and vodka. But I couldn't stop thinking, *Why am I alive? Why am I here?* A new life I never owned was slipping away from me, fading into an abyss. Even in my darkest hour, death wouldn't take me. Now where was I to turn?

I'd later learn that many of the children I'd heard about who grew up in the Children of God and attempted suicide had, unlike me, succeeded.

Mom and Dad found my suicide note and took me to lunch at Subway to talk about it. I had never been out alone with just my parents. There's an embarrassment that comes with a failed attempt at suicide, and there's no real way to explain it to anyone, much less to the people who gave you life. The day was grey and overcast.

"So, do you want to talk?" Dad said, unwrapping his sub. I sat across from them with my arms folded across my chest and didn't say a word. I didn't know how to address the topic with my parents. Father David had never talked about suicide or the desire to want to kill oneself. When his son Aaron jumped off a cliff in Switzerland soon after the Children of God was founded and he went mad, Father David told his followers that Aaron had gone to a mountaintop to be with God, like Moses. We, too, were all going to die willingly at the Great Apocalypse, a death

I could never fully prepare for. But the topic of suicide and its consequences—whether it was a sin or a noble act—was never mentioned in the Family.

"Flor, you know we love you, don't you?" Mom said. She put her hand on mine. Her skin was rough and her fingers wrinkled, the same way they had been when she came to my bed at night to comfort me and tape Bible verses to my wall because I was paralyzed with fear over the End Time. "We would never do anything to hurt you or any of your brothers and sisters," she said.

"I know," I said. I looked down at the pile of chips I had dumped on my napkin, but I wasn't hungry. I knew it was much more complicated than love.

"And we tried our best," Mom said. "We raised you the best way we knew how."

"I know you did," I said. "I know you love us. It's just. . . ." I looked away and felt hot tears welling up. I blinked them back and wiped my face with the cuff of my jacket. They would never understand.

"Is Tamar okay?" Mom asked.

"Tamar's fine," I said. I didn't want to talk about it anymore.

They never asked why I did it or addressed the suicide question directly, but as hard as I tried I couldn't find the words to tell them. Nor did I bring up the topic of the Children of God. They would never understand the connection, if indeed there was one. It was an awkward lunch with lots of silence and unexplained tears over a dry tuna salad sandwich.

My parents were adults when they made the decision to join the Children of God. It had been their choice to bring their kids into the fold. But as the Family progressed and changed, the adults—not just the children—were abandoned and cheated and manipulated and lied to. Our parents had to leave for trainings even if they didn't want to. Mom later told me how she wanted nothing more than to be with us kids and often felt conflicted about being separated from us, especially when we were very young. She and Dad had lost most of their contact with the external world and would have had a hard time leaving even if they'd wanted to. I found out later that shortly after we moved to Thailand, the leadership of the Family, suspicious of my parents' thriving mail ministry, had begun to monitor their contact with outside sponsors and donors, thus controlling my parents' financial resources and communication with the outside world. Maybe my parents never wanted to be in a cult, I wondered. Maybe, like me, they just couldn't get out. They would never understand my experience, I reasoned. They were still figuring out their own.

■ ■

A FEW WEEKS AFTER MY failed attempt at suicide, I was kicked out of Rowland High School for carrying vodka in my backpack while on my way home from school. Since I hadn't yet arrived at my destination, I was technically still on "school property," I learned from the officer who searched my bag. He explained that because I was fifteen they couldn't officially arrest me, but my expulsion basically counted as an arrest. It was early December, just before my sixteenth birthday, and school was almost out for winter break.

The following semester I was mandated to attend Rowland Community Day School, located down the block from the main high school campus in a cluster of portable wood-paneled grey buildings with sky-blue trim. For the first time in our lives, Tamar and I were no longer together all the time. A sense of relief accompanied the solitude of being an individual instead of a twin and the inevitable spectacle that came with it. I knew I would miss Tamar, but I was also happy to be away from the social pressure of high school and the temptation to get high every day.

I looked around the room. All the other kids were either black or Hispanic. I was the only white person besides the teacher, Mrs. Watson, who had frizzy blond hair and fair skin. My class was the only one with girls, and Helen was the only other girl besides me who had gotten expelled from school—in her case, for beating up another girl in a gang fight. The other buildings had classrooms full of rowdy boys who were there for drug offenses or gang fights or other serious breaches of school code.

I wasn't sure I wanted to go back to regular high school, but I decided I'd still do my best. I had nothing to lose. I found that I liked the obscurity and routine offered by community school, even though the class work was easy. I had been kicked out of Rowland High School with a 4.0 GPA. Although I didn't comprehend the consequences of having good grades, I had intentionally kept my grades up despite my other failures. Schoolwork was one thing that was easy for me.

Every day Mrs. Watson gave us a sheet of paper with a crossword puzzle or fill-in-the-blank problems. Because most of the kids in my class had trouble with school and were either failing or getting Ds, I was assigned to work with a mentor since I had potential as a student and was capable of being redeemed, Mrs. Watson said. She never used those exact words, but I could tell she had hope in me. She talked to me like I was her equal, not her inferior. She told me if I kept up my attendance at community school and didn't mess up or get arrested again, I could go back to Rowland High School in a year.

"You know, some kids never go back to their campus," she said. "But I believe in you. You can do it."

One day Mrs. Watson asked me if I had ever considered going to college. I didn't dare tell her about my past or that I'd never thought of college. Father David said colleges were just centers for arrogant phonies and intellectual know-it-alls. But Mrs. Watson was speaking my language, a language of hope.

After the obligatory year at community school, I was allowed to attend classes on campus again. Because I had aced the easy in-class work at community school, I was set to graduate a year early. Tamar was also doing better in her studies. After our being separated for that year, something inside me had calmed. Because we were apart most of the time, we weren't able to go on drunken brawls or shoplifting sprees or hang out with our so-called friends after school. The change in environment gave me a new sense of confidence; I was slowly gaining a sense of self. I realized I was worth more than what I had been taught. *Self-esteem.* The words were becoming a new part of my psyche. This awareness came simply from spending time alone. As a child, I had always been surrounded by people, bombarded with Father David's teachings, and burdened with saving the world. Now, for the first time, I was getting to know myself.

CHAPTER 32

MOM AND DAD WERE NO longer part of the Family, in large part because dealing with Mom's cancer diagnosis had taken priority over their commitment to Father David's doctrines. My parents hadn't been excommunicated, the way adults in earlier days might have been had their commitment wavered, but their decisions to seek traditional medical treatment and to send their kids to public school no longer aligned with the teachings of the Family. They never discussed what it was like to leave; they merely said they were trying to do what was best for us. For a while they maintained contact with some members and received occasional letters with updates.

Without the leadership of Father David, the Family continued to fall apart. Stories of kids who had left the Family and committed suicide shortly after kept emerging, which saddened me. Mostly they were young people whose parents had stayed in the Family. I had never been abused the way some of the other second-generation members had been, and although I had unsuccessfully attempted to take my life, at least now I had some support from my parents and sisters. We had struggles, but we were in it together and each coping in our own way. It helped that our parents didn't send us out into the world alone but decided to leave with us.

■ ■

I HAD JUST TURNED SEVENTEEN and was about to graduate from Rowland High School. Dad had enrolled in community college—another life choice that would have been forbidden by the Family leadership in the old days—and was working toward a degree in kinesiology. All the credits he'd earned at UC Davis toward a degree in geology before joining the Children of God were worth nothing, so he had decided to start over, complete his bachelor's degree, and become a high school PE teacher. John had a full-time salaried job in refrigeration with General Electric and lived in a two-bedroom apartment in Huntington Beach. Tamar was dating a nice boy she'd met in math class. I was also in a relationship that was good for me and boosted my self-confidence. Mary Ann had started a part-time gig walking dogs on weekdays. Heidi was still hanging out with her goth friends. She, William, and the rest of the middle kids were in grade school, a routine I was completely unfamiliar with. Mom was in recovery from her cancer treatment and stayed home full-time to take care of our youngest siblings.

We also had a new family business as clowns. Many members of the Family had gotten into clowning—or live music—when the Children of God started to splinter. Performing was one of the few things for which we needed no academic qualifications, and we were used to singing and dancing for systemite groups to raise money. Many clown troupes sprung up in the U.S. in the aftermath of Father David's death.

Our clown business thrived. We had official-looking business cards made with curly blue letters spelling out our group's name: "Family of Clowns." I looked forward to the weekends because it meant that for two days I could be somebody other than myself. Dad studied during the week, but on weekends he dressed up as a clown and drove out to Del Amo mall in Torrance to make animal balloons in exchange for tips in front of Forever 21. That, along with government assistance, provided enough to live on. Mary Ann, Tamar, and I worked as clowns on weekends at malls, farmers' markets, and private parties. Most weekends we raked in $300 per person per day.

■ ■

ONE DAY IN LATE SPRING Tamar came home and announced with glee, "Flor! Four years. Four years is all it takes." She threw down her purse and rushed over to where I was sitting on the stone bench that wrapped around the fireplace.

"Have you ever thought about going to college?" she asked me.

I had never seen her so thrilled. I perked up. Aside from my brief conversation with Mrs. Watson at community school, I hadn't given college much thought.

"Flor! We can become stewardesses. Four years is all it takes!"

Because we had never heard about college, Tamar was under the impression that a two-year college degree was required to become a flight attendant when really it would only take a few weeks. Mostly, she was excited about the prospect of attending college and was determined that was our course of study. She handed me a course catalog from Mt. San Antonio College, a community college that sat at the foothills of Mount Baldy. She opened it and pointed to a list of flight-attendance courses.

"We get to take other classes too, and we can even transfer somewhere else if we want to," she said excitedly.

I took the book from her and looked it over. It was true. There were courses in English, math, electives in everything from Spanish to horticulture to dance.

"Flor, imagine! We could attend a university! There's a campus in Malibu that overlooks the ocean," she said ecstatically. "It's called Pepperdine, and it's *beautiful!*"

Father David had said education was evil, universities were places of sin and corruption, and the professors who pretended to know everything were a bunch of phonies. Now, if I wanted to, maybe I could travel the world and get paid to ask people, "Would you like ice with your soda?" Or, "Would you like your peanuts honey-roasted or salted?" I imagined us with our hair tied back in tight ponytails, dressed in matching navy blue outfits with white buttons and floppy ties, chic black stockings, and little high heels clicking as we walked down the narrow aisles.

Soon I was just as excited as Tamar was. For the first time in my life, I had an inkling that I could do something and be somebody.

CHAPTER 33

TAMAR AND I ENROLLED IN community college the next fall. I hadn't finished all the credits I needed to complete high school, but that didn't matter. We had to start at the beginning in most subjects, taking prerequisites as stepping stones to college courses—pre-algebra, algebra, and finally college algebra. We didn't have a car—or even driver's licenses—so to simplify transportation we enrolled in the same classes. We shared textbooks to save money, and we decided to major in the same subject: business. The only class where we differed was English. Tamar enrolled in beginning composition, but I did well on my placement test, making me eligible for freshman composition.

In English class I read my first real novel, *The Tortilla Curtain*, by T. C. Boyle, and wrote my first essay. Every time I sat down to write, something magical happened: my mind transformed from confused and chaotic to clear, organized, and sometimes even witty. I was transported to a place of no-time and no-mind, and it was a good feeling. I was no longer thinking; I was just doing. Sometimes the words came faster than I could keep up. I began to realize I had a mind capable of making decisions and forming ideas. I could have opinions; more importantly, I was free to express them. And I was kind of good at it. Is this what freedom felt like? I excelled in trigonometry, calculus, philosophy, Spanish, and economics. I regularly made the dean's list.

For our final project, my English professor, Ron Brouilette, who had curly hair and circular glasses, assigned a ten-page research paper on any topic of our choice. I had this one in the bag. As I started to write I discovered my childhood was a gold mine for material, no longer a piece of my past weighing me down. It had color and texture. Darkness and tragedy too, but most of all I had *something* to work with. Like a potter uses clay, I had material with which to form stories. When I wrote, I had a voice, something I never had growing up.

I began to realize that my mind was the most powerful tool I possessed, and all my life it had been controlled by a man who claimed to be the voice of God. The thought enraged me. It was something Tamar and I talked about. On some days, instead of taking the bus or waiting for Dad to pick us up, we walked the seven miles home from campus down Lemon Avenue through hilly residential neighborhoods lined with rows of willows and pepper trees. We talked about Father David. We talked about our family. We shared memories from childhood, but the lens through which we viewed it now was crystal clear; we understood what had happened. We did research and read books and understood what *cult* meant. We read articles on the Children of God and saw it from the outside. We watched documentaries. Unlike some of our childhood friends who blamed their circumstances on the past, we decided we wouldn't be victims.

I tried to blame my parents, but I couldn't. When my sisters and I decided we wanted out that day at Lake Tahoe, they decided to leave with us. My parents put us kids first in the best way they knew how, and I chose to forgive them.

We had never been able to ask or answer the question "What do you want to be when you grow up?" Now we were doing that, and with it came the prospect of a future.

The cool autumn air combined with my long talks with Tamar began to turn something in me. Through conversation I found a way to narrate my story; through language we patched up the holes in our past. By telling the story to each other we began to understand and find meaning in it, and now we had the language to discuss it with our friends. We started to talk about our past, something we were never comfortable doing in high school. We found our peers in college more open-minded. They were intrigued. We relished the attention. I was beginning to understand the power of a story. I *wanted* to tell my story. And I wanted to tell it through writing. I titled my research paper "The Family of Love: A Cult."

"I hope you enjoy my paper," I told Mr. Brouilette triumphantly as I turned it in. "One day I'm going to write a book!" He nodded, looked at me through his round reading glasses, and didn't say a word. I got an A in the class.

■ ■

SOON IT WAS TIME TO transfer from Mt. San Antonio College. In our last semester there, students rushed to and fro finishing exams and submitting applications to four-year universities. We had honors economics with Amrik Singh Dhua, who had a calm presence and a gentle smile under his delicate mustache. All the

students in the class were Asian except for Tamar and me and a
white boy who was transferring to Biola University, a Christian
institution. Tamar and I made it a point never to look into their
curriculum. Christianity and all things God-related had become
a curse that we avoided like the plague. One day, Mr. Dhua
announced that because of our class's excellent academic status,
the college had offered to fund a field trip for the whole group
to UC Berkeley. If we wanted to go, all we had to do was sign up.
They'd take care of travel, accommodations, and a tour. He passed
around a sign-up sheet.

I raised my hand. "What's UC Berkeley?" I heard the room gasp.

"UC Berkeley is in the East Bay—one of the best schools in
America," Mr. Dhua answered, waving his hand at a map of California tacked to the wall.

I didn't want to ask where the East Bay was and decided I
would research it later. I looked at Tamar and gave her a nod. We
covered our mouths and chuckled like we did when we were kids
and weren't allowed to laugh.

■ ■

I WAS EIGHTEEN GOING ON nineteen. I was supposed to be
dead. And I had my whole life ahead of me. Everyone told me I
was smart, even exceptional. I felt different from others, but being
different didn't seem to get you anywhere in this world. The tour
guide at UC Berkeley, a double major in French and English with
spiky red hair and intelligent-looking glasses, said, "UC Berkeley
likes diversity. It's all about your personal statement."

Tamar and I decided to apply. I struggled to write my personal
statement. Do I say I grew up in a cult in Thailand? Or that I was
the child of missionaries doing charity work "overseas"? Do I
tell them I don't have a high school diploma, that I never went

to grade school, *and* that I read my first real novel when I was seventeen? Shall I tell them all the things I have seen? Do I dare mention Father David? He was becoming a ghostly sliver of my past, slowly disappearing into the deep archives of my memory. No. I decided to save that for the book I'd told Mr. Brouilette I would write.

I had Tamar proofread my essay.

"You left a lot out," she said.

"I know. I had to."

■ ■

THE NEXT SPRING TWO IDENTICAL letters arrived in the mail. It was late afternoon, and I was sitting on the sofa, drinking my afternoon green tea with Tamar and watching *Oprah*. Outside, a light shower fell.

I read my letter alone in my room. I'd been accepted. So had Tamar. I heard her excitedly telling Mom and Dad the news. I thought about what it meant. Tamar and I had lived our whole lives together, spending more time with each other than most people could spend with another. "Known each other since before birth," we'd often say. We had shared experiences most people would never understand or could even imagine.

I looked out the window. A butterfly landed softly on a nearby hydrangea. The air smelled fresh and damp. The rain had subsided, and clouds were parting in the grey sky in an unstoppable dance that filled me with hope. Sunset had arrived, and a sharp golden light split through a layer of low silver clouds that had settled near the distant mountaintops.

I put the letter down, took a deep breath, and walked toward the door.

EPILOGUE

ONE COLD JANUARY AFTERNOON, WHILE I was still attending Mt. San Antonio College, I came home after a long day of sitting in classes. Besides English, history had become one of my favorite subjects. I loved hearing stories about how this country was founded. All I knew from my childhood lessons was the story of the Boston Tea Party as told by Father David in his comic books. He used it to illustrate how the United States was built on corruption and greed and would be the first in line for God's judgment come the Great Apocalypse.

It was raining. Mom was cooking dinner.

"Did you hear the news?" she said while submerging a dimpled chicken into a pot of boiling water.

I shook off my umbrella. "What news?"

"Davidito killed himself. He took his life after stabbing his ex-babysitter to death. It's all over the TV."

Davidito had been our role model when we were children, the appointed heir to Father David's throne. We were taught to strive to be like him. His murder/suicide sent shock waves through those who'd grown up in the Children of God.

Young people who had killed themselves after leaving the Family usually blamed their parents for not teaching them basic survival skills, like how to write checks or fill out applications or hold their own in a normal social setting. I'd heard about girls who became strippers because although they knew how to give the so-called Look of Love, they had no other skills for working or making money. I wasn't sure if my success in making it so far was an accident or partly due to my own tenacity and will. Or maybe it was because of my parents, who left with me, or because I had a twin, someone to whom I could talk. Either way, I felt lucky.

That night I turned on the news. *60 Minutes* and the other shows were running specials on Davidito. They described him as an ex–cult member from a mysterious secret society. He had left a transcribed videotape of his spiteful plans. For the first time, I watched events from the outside as they happened in real time. Montel Williams and Dr. Phil each ran previews of a "cult special" that would feature ex-members of the Children of God. They showed clips from videos of the early days: topless women dancing in circles, young girls putting on a hot Hawaiian number for Father David, the hallucinatory prayer meetings, homes in Argentina filled with tired kids marching to their duties like soldiers in a war.

The TV screen also showed "top secret" videos of a bearded Father David sitting in his black bathrobe with a Bible in hand and a cross dangling from his neck. A backdrop of palm trees was painted on the wall so it would look like he was in a tropical paradise. But really he was in hiding.

■ ■

I WENT TO VISIT JOHN. He stood on the doorstep of his apartment smoking a cigarette and drinking a beer. His black hair was slicked back. His skin was darker than usual, and his face broke into a grin when he saw me.

"You look tan," I said.

"Yeah, I've been to the tanning salon," he said.

"Why?" I asked. "You're already so dark."

"It helps me with the ladies," he said, slapping his palm in the air.

I told him about an article I was writing for my class and how my professor thought it was a good story. Whenever I talk to John about our childhood, he always made a point to defend our parents.

"Our parents had good intentions," he said. "In the beginning they were just trying to help people. That's all. They wanted to be missionaries."

He paused for a moment. It was late afternoon, and the sun was disappearing behind a curtain of pink clouds above the San Gabriel Mountains. City lights began to twinkle.

"In a way they kind of did," he said. "I mean, we helped people. I remember going to orphanages and giving things to people and singing. . . and helping. We did help people," he said with conviction.

"Yeah, I remember that part too," I said. And I did.

I can still see in my mind's eye the pictures of John looking into the camera with his signature smile—beaming eyes and perfect teeth—holding the shriveled hand of an old, frail Thai woman after a flood had wiped away all of her belongings.

"Things just got weird with all the loving-Jesus-hallelujah hoopla," he said.

I thought about how people who joined the Children of God were looking for a way out of their ordinary lives. Although I didn't agree with what they did, I understood an inner urge had pushed them to drop everything, including family and friends, to join a group that promised them something more than their worldly existence could provide. They were people of action and passion. I don't know that I would have made the same choices they did, but I could empathize with them now, especially after having had my own negative experiences with the "outside" world. I was starting to see what they had wanted to escape from. They were trying to escape a life of mundanity, the illusion of the American Dream.

"I think things got weird once we kids came along," I said. "They had to find a way to control us." I thought about how control, like jealousy, works the exact opposite way you want it to. Gaining control over oneself and one's decisions after a lifetime in captivity is just another opportunity for freedom, and the only way I could free myself was through words, which is why I wanted to be a writer. "They turned a hippie-sex-wannabe-missionary movement into a children's training boot camp."

John snuffed out his cigarette in a quarter-empty beer bottle on the deck's railing.

"When I meet people I can't even begin to tell them about my past," he said. "I don't know where to start. It's so complex." His dark eyes became a well of suppressed memories.

"I know," I said.

We agreed that it was especially tough with boyfriends or girl-friends. We talked about how it takes a long time to open up to another person because of our history.

"The past will always haunt you," I said. I looked into the last streaks of orange and pink clouds reflecting the sun that had just disappeared behind the low hills.

"People just don't understand," he said.

Our parents were still recovering—even all these years later—from the aftermath of Father David's death and their subsequent abandonment. When I ask Dad about it, he says it's an open wound, especially the time when Mom was sick.

I fiddled with a shriveled leaf that had fallen off a nearby fig tree.

"Do you still believe in God?" I asked.

"Yeah, I guess I do," John said. "I still pray. . . sometimes."

"I think Jesus was a good man," I said. "I think humans messed things up by interpreting his words. Maybe Jesus never meant to start a religion. I distrust 'interpreters like Father David,' I told John when he came back. "I think God can be a dangerous word.

While John went inside to get another beer, I wrestled with the questions these conversations always brought up for me. I could find no solace. The sun became a sliver behind the horizon.

■ ■

IT WAS 2005 WHEN DAVIDITO died. He was called Ricky Rodriguez in those days. As they had been in the 1970s when the cult was started and again in 1995 when it fell apart, the major news outlets were once again saturated with stories of the Children of God. The Children of God had had a long and complicated history with the media. If I didn't tell my story, I decided, reporters were going to keep spinning it into a narrative of sensationalism and controversy, victims and villains. One day I made a resolution: I was going to get to that book I told myself I would write. *I* was going to shape the narrative of my life. I was going to take back my childhood, and writing it was the only way I knew how.

After spending time teaching in Costa Rica and Bangkok, I visited my parents while looking into graduate writing programs. They still lived in the house in Diamond Bar with the magnificent view of the San Gabriel Valley. Aside from a few new housing developments in the nearby hills, everything looked the same. There was the steady stream of lights where the 60 ran east and west. There was the Hollywood sign in the distance, hiding behind a thick blanket of smog. There was Mount Baldy to the right with patches of snow in its topmost crevices. In the center basin of the valley sat my high school, with its familiar blue and red walls, fenced-in track field, and deep-blue swimming pool. It was where I'd had my first experience with the world I'd been sheltered from.

I stood on the deck that Dad had spent months renovating earlier that year, installing heavy floorboards and painting the railing with thick coats of varnish. Rain fell lightly. Memories were beginning to abound. I sat in the canopy swing that Mom had bought to add a homely touch to our awkward house. The awning shielded me from the rain.

I picked up a pen, and I started to write.